Four Faces of Truth

Four Faces of Truth

BY

Harriette C. Rinaldi

www.Fireshippress.com

Four Faces of Truth by Harriette C. Rinaldi

Copyright © 2014 Harriette C. Rinaldi

ISBN-13: 978-1-61179-313-0 (Paperback)
ISBN: 978-1-61179-314-7 (e-book)

BISAC Subject Headings:
HIS048000 HISTORY / Asia / Southeast Asia
FIC037000 FICTION / Political
POL061000 POLITICAL SCIENCE / Genocide & War Crimes

Cover photo by Barry Broman.

Cover work by Christine Horner

Address all correspondence to:
Fireship Press, LLC
P.O. Box 68412
Tucson, AZ 85737
Or visit our website at:
www.fireshippress.com

Disclaimer

All statements of fact, opinion, or analysis expressed are those of the author and do not reflect the official positions or views of the CIA or any other U.S. Government agency. Nothing in the contents should be construed as asserting or implying U.S Government authentication of information or Agency endorsement of the author's views. This material has been reviewed by the CIA to prevent the disclosure of classified information.

Dedication

For Larry Bourassa, Reverend Philip D. McNamara, and all international aid workers who served in Cambodia and in Thai refugee camps in the 1970s and 1980s.

Table of Contents

Reviews

Four Faces of Truth is a poignant, fictionalized account of Cambodia's tumultuous history since World War II as seen through the eyes of four skillfully imagined participant observers. In these pages, Ms Rinaldi displays an enviable "feel" for the ways Cambodians think and behave and a talent for capturing the essence of what millions of Cambodians have recently endured. In *Four Faces of Truth* she has constructed a darkly tinted, multi-faceted narrative that is very moving and very persuasive.

David Chandler, Monash University
Author of A History of Cambodia *(4th edition 2007).*
Brother Number One: A Political Biography of Pol Pot.

Harriette Rinaldi has written a magic novel of modern Cambodian history. Like all good historical fiction, it uses the facts together with the vicissitudes of her very well-drawn characters to portray the horrors of Khmer Rouge Cambodia. She vividly depicts the roots of Cambodian communism in the personalities of the major figures. This book wonderfully rebuts the nonsense of "gentle" Cambodians. It makes plain how and why the Khmer Rouge regime happened.

Ambassador Tim Carney,
Director of UN Transitional Authority in Cambodia,
Director for Asian Affairs on National Security Staff,
author of Whither Cambodia? Beyond the Election

Using fiction to bring 1970s Cambodia alive, Harriette Rinaldi demonstrates through the use of four compelling narrators, just how the murderous Khmer Rouge regime took hold in that country. This book keenly tracks the trajectory of Cambodia as it slides into the abyss of war and genocide. The interplay of four distinct voices, along with Rinaldi's first-hand knowledge of Cambodia, gives the story its depth. While each narrator's story is unique, all are woven together flawlessly. Rinaldi takes us right into the maelstrom of the revolution led by Pol Pot, whose wife continues to slip into the paranoid schizophrenia that would consume her. Cambodia itself is present like another character, alive with amazingly diverse natural resources and unique architectural treasures.

Judy Ledgerwood,
Director for Southeast Asian Studies and
Professor, Department of Anthropology,
Northern Illinois University

Preface

Why this book? Why now—almost forty years since the Khmer Rouge seized power in Cambodia? When I mention the words Khmer Rouge or the name Pol Pot, the most frequent reaction I receive is a blank stare of non-recognition. When the Khmer Rouge were plotting their revolution and eventually overthrowing the government of Prime Minister Lon Nol, America was focused on extricating itself from its failed military involvement in neighboring Vietnam and reeling from the Watergate scandal and the impeachment of President Richard Nixon. Because Cambodia was not the victim of a major natural disaster, to which the rest of the world usually responds with great outpourings of sympathy or support, the sufferings of its people are still largely ignored today. Yet, millions died at the hands of the Khmer Rouge, and tens of thousands remain traumatized by the horrors they experienced. I wrote this book because there are too many parallels and lessons from that period of history that apply to what is happening in many parts of the world today.

In the course of my twenty-seven-year career with the Central Intelligence Agency, I served in Phnom Penh from 1972 to 1975. Despite the ongoing war between government forces and the Khmer Rouge, I was able to travel to government-controlled provinces throughout the country where I observed the beauty and diversity of Cambodia's natural resources, as well as the harmful effects of that war on the Khmer people.

After Pol Pot began his reign of terror in 1975, I had the unexpected opportunity to meet Khmer Rouge Foreign Minister Ieng Sary and his wife Ieng Thirith, who was also a Khmer Rouge cabinet minister. Thirith was the sister of Khieu Ponnary, the wife of Pol Pot. Like Sary and Thirith, I studied at the Sorbonne in Paris and was able to communicate with them, based on a common language and experience.

Historians have produced volumes about the Pol Pot era, but these are largely inaccessible to the lay reader. Many survivors of the Khmer Rouge reign of terror have written heart-wrenching accounts of their suffering. Unfortunately, these overwhelming litanies of pain are often devoid of any wider historical context. My goal in writing this book was to present this tragic story in a way that enables the lay reader to understand not only the torment inflicted on the Cambodian people by the demonic Pol Pot, but also the overarching political and cultural influences that led to the rise of the Khmer Rouge.

I believe the best vehicle for presenting this information to lay readers is through the eyes of plausible fictional narrators who can place events in the context of Cambodia's history and culture, while at the same time communicating the drama and pathos of what they saw and experienced.

Why *Four Faces of Truth*? Each of my four fictional narrators presents and represents a specific view into the rise of the Khmer Rouge and the damage done to Cambodia by a handful of Paris-educated young people intent on creating a communist utopia—but who went on instead to murder over two million of their fellow countrymen, destroying much of Cambodia's cultural heritage in the process. These compelling narrators expand our understanding of the era and the key players involved:

Hem Narong (The General and the Buddha), a former Buddhist monk serving as an aide to General Lon Nol, realizes how the General's failure as a leader paves the way for the rise of the Khmer Rouge.

Thoun Sophana (Sophana's Story), a well-educated young woman and enthusiastic member of the nascent Khmer communist movement, is betrayed by the revolution she once supported.

Eng Maly (Mother of the Revolution), a practitioner of traditional Chinese medicine, she treats Pol Pot's wife Ponnary, who is essential to the success of the revolution but suffers from chronic paranoid schizophrenia.

Marcel Blanchette (Patriacide), a western archeologist restoring ancient Khmer temples, witnesses the damage done by the Khmer Rouge to Cambodia's architectural heritage and natural resources.

While each of these narrators presents the Khmer Rouge regime from a different perspective, their lives often intersect and their stories form a unified mosaic portraying the suffering of the Khmer people under Pol Pot. Peace, light, and beauty were smashed, distorted, and transformed into darkness and horror, like a living depiction of the abomination expressed a generation earlier in Picasso's *Guernica*.

Viewing events from four points of view also seems in keeping with traditional Khmer symbolism and artistic expression. When the great King Jayavarman VII (1181–c.1220) built the Buddhist-inspired monuments of Angkor Thom, he created immense stone towers crowned with four faces, each looking out toward a different geographic direction. One guide at Angkor described these serene countenances as "faces of truth" that have borne witness to all the good and all the evil that have occurred within Cambodia's borders over the centuries. The four narrators presented here also represent faces of truth compelling readers to listen and learn from what they have witnessed.

Bleed, bleed, poor country!
Our country sinks beneath the yoke [of the tyrant].
It weeps, it bleeds, and each day a new gash
Is added to her wounds.
Not in the legions
Of horrid hell can come a devil more damned
In evils to top [this man].
Bloody, malicious, smacking of every sin
That has a name. But there's no bottom, none.
Alas! Poor country;
Almost afraid to know itself. It cannot
Be called our mother, but our grave.

—excerpts from Shakespeare's *Macbeth*
Act 4, Scene 3

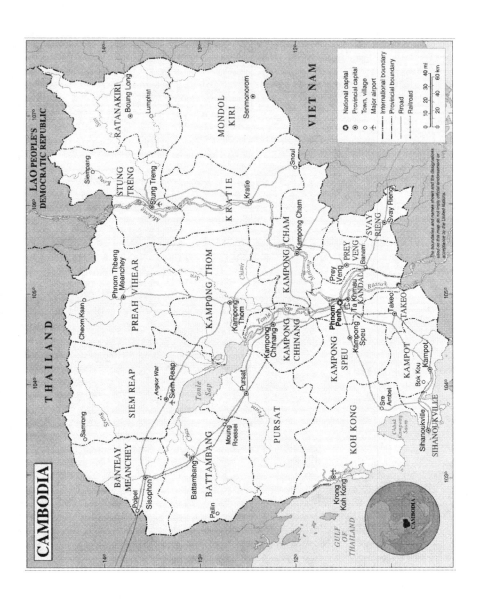

Chapter 1

The General and the Buddha

by Hem Narong

General Lon Nol was haunted until his death by forces he unwittingly unleashed after taking part in the overthrow of Prince Norodom Sihanouk. Worse yet, the General was terrified that the *karma* he had created in his lifetime foreshadowed future lives of abomination for himself and his descendants. When I accompanied the General into exile after the Khmer Rouge victory in 1975, I often observed him weeping and revisiting his transgressions against the precepts of the Buddha.

I met the General in 1959, when I was eighteen years old, after having spent ten years in a Buddhist monastery in my home province of Battambang. I was confused and unsure whether I wanted to become a monk, but had no idea what else to do with my life. My mother, who had become a close friend of Lon Nol's wife while he served as Governor of Battambang Province, wrote to her friend and asked if I could be of service to her husband who, by that time, had become the head of Prince Sihanouk's Army and National Police. I was apprehensive about leaving the peaceful countryside of Battambang and entering an urban existence that was so alien to my own, but my mother said that my experience in the monastery was exactly what the General would value in a member of his staff. The General's wife explained to my mother that her husband did not wish to surround himself solely with intellectuals or those who did not value our Buddhist traditions.

In looking back over my years in service to the General (of all the titles he eventually assumed, that of General was his favorite), I recall vividly our first conversation in which he interviewed me for a position on his staff. As he entered the room where I was waiting, the General asked me a series of questions.

"Young man, what is your favorite story about the Buddha?"

"I always loved the story about his birth, when the heavens and earth showed signs: the dumb spoke, the lame walked, and all men began to speak kindly. At that moment, musical instruments played by themselves, the earth was covered with lotus flowers, lotuses descended from the skies, and every tree put forth its flowers."

"What is the difference between Prince Sihanouk and other men?"

"Just as there are powerful spirits that inhabit the forests and mountains, there are even more potent spirits that inhabit the universe. These more powerful spirits, or energies, flow down to the earth to protect those chosen by the Buddha to rule the Khmer people. That is why our beloved Prince Norodom Sihanouk, or *Samdech Euv* (Milord Daddy) as we call him, possesses the radiant energy of the Buddha in abundance. Other men are not worthy to look upon or touch such people. The kings chosen by the Buddha own all the land. We, the children of *Samdech Euv,* owe our livelihood, allegiance, and loyalty to him."

"Do you believe in harmful or evil spirits as well, my son?"

"Yes, sir. Like the stars at certain times of the astrological year, spirits can cause evil things to happen. *Neak ta* (spirits) exist everywhere. If we honor them, they will be beneficial; if we do not, they can cause us harm. Whenever I enter a forest, I share my first meal with the *neak ta* who live there. Likewise, I would never cut down a tree without first calling upon and making an offering to the spirit that inhabits the tree. Large stones and mountains are also the abodes of *neak ta,* in whose good graces we must remain. Whenever certain diseases afflict people, we should honor the spirits that cause those diseases. My family always paid homage to the beneficial spirits who protect the house from evil ones."

"What do you think of the *yuon*, my son?" Because of his hatred for his neighbors to the east, Lon Nol never used the word "Vietnamese" but rather chose *yuon*, a term that means the lowest form of life.

"They are *thmil*, or infidels. Throughout our history, we have been humiliated and crushed by these people who are filled with evil spirits. They refer to the Khmer as crude people, and mock our dark skins."

"Narong, my son, I am pleased to tell you that I have chosen you to serve as one of my personal aides. Your knowledge of the Buddha and loyalty to our great leader, Prince Norodom Sihanouk, prove to me that I can trust you. When you are in my household, I entreat you to call me by the name used by my troops when they address me. That name, which honors the nature of the dark-skinned Khmer people, is Ta Khmao (Black Papa)."

****

Over the years that I served on his staff, the General spent many hours explaining to his aides the importance of our Khmer traditions and wisdom. He gave similar lectures to his officers and troops during his infrequent visits to the field, even though this was difficult for him. When he spoke to any audience, no matter how small, he was uncomfortable and visibly shy. He looked away or down at his notes instead of looking others in the eye. Although he had many good qualities, he did not excel at public speaking. Because of his shyness, he preferred to send messages by letter rather than in person. I believe he was the only one of Sihanouk's officials who would not appear in the Prince's films.

Sometimes, when talking about Buddhism or the great kings of Angkor, the General seemed to enter a trance-like state. There were long pauses; his voice usually trailed off; and it became difficult to hear all that he was saying. Sometimes he spoke in French, and sometimes in our own language. Whenever he did speak in French, he loved to use particularly flowery French phrases he had learned at the French schools.

I still have the journal where I began copying out the many lessons the General gave his staff members concerning Khmer history and culture so that I could better understand the man I served. Even though these words of General Lon Nol may not be completely accurate, I can state with confidence that they represent as closely as possible what I heard him say many times in his slow, halting manner.

Our Khmer civilization was the most important, the most brilliant, and the most original of ancient Indochina. Reminders of the glory of our civilization are found today in the powerful monuments built by the kings of Angkor. We originally belonged to the large ethnic family known as the Mon-Khmer. The kingdom known to the Chinese as Funan, which extended from Indochina to the Malay Peninsula, was conquered in the seventh century by the kingdom of Chenla. The fusion of these two great kingdoms under Jayavarman I formed the powerful Khmer dynasty, which expanded to include Burma, Laos, and Thailand.

There are those today who deride our history, claiming that the Khmer civilization is like a beautiful but barren tree that will die, unlike those civilizations that flourish, bear fruit, and spread their culture to other lands. But it is within our power to ensure the viability of our culture and the continuation of Buddhism for at least a thousand more years.

Above all, be wary of the *yuon*. Like our ancestors, we must take forceful measures to repel them from our territory. Do not forget the harm they have caused us. Once, in the mid-nineteenth century, an occupying *yuon* general ordered his troops to behead four or five Khmer citizens on an imperative from the *yuon* emperor. The troops used these poor victims' heads to support the boiler pot for making the general's tea.

At other times, the General lectured us on his philosophy of work and on obedience to one's superiors. The following are two examples that may disturb some readers today, especially those not familiar with Cambodian culture:

> We have as much respect for an official who does little work but earns millions of *riels*, as we do for a man who toils from dawn to dusk and makes barely enough to survive. We can dance or eat anytime during the day or night, and combine study or work time with break or play time. I can use a government car for official work as well as for personal reasons, such as transporting my wife, children, or mistresses.
>
> Ancient proverbs tell us, "When we believe in someone, we believe in them one hundred and twenty percent. If you drink, then drink so much that others have to carry you out. If you kill someone, go ahead and taste the flesh." That is why I tell my soldiers and officers, "Go ahead and eat the livers of those you destroy. Their strength will enhance your strength."

As I re-read these words I had heard so many times while in the General's service, I wonder whether readers might ask if these references to violent and immoral behavior distressed me. Quite the contrary; these statements reflected attitudes and beliefs with which I was already familiar and did not disturb me at all.

When I was a child, my father died while fighting against a branch of the Khmer Issarak (Free Khmer) that advocated independence from France and the overthrow of the monarchy, and killed their enemies with extreme cruelty. Because his body was never recovered, my mother told me that her greatest fear was that the Issarak may have removed my father's liver and eaten it because he was a particularly strong warrior.

References to acts of brutality and unswerving allegiance to one's promise to a person in authority abound in the folk tales I learned as a child. In one of these, known as The Golden Arrow, a king declares that he will use this arrow to kill anyone who interferes with his war plan. When he discovers that his beloved queen has looked at the plan in his absence, he knows what he must do. He kills her with the golden arrow.

Over the years, I tried to understand the deep contradictions of Lon Nol's nature, which reflected both the gentle and violent aspects of what one could call the Khmer temperament. I recognized his sincere but imperfect attempts to follow the teachings of Buddha. I had much greater respect for the actions and temperament of his first wife, to whom I owed my position on the General's staff. When I think of her strong spirit, I cannot help but recall the proverb that "a senseless man usually has a wife of excellent quality."

Because the General and his first wife had no children, she treated me like a son, regularly sought me out to ask about my welfare, and kept my mother informed of my progress on her husband's staff. With her firm but smiling manner, she was able to bend the General to her will, and she had a major influence on official decisions made by her husband. While Westerners may not understand this, women have traditionally played important roles in our society. We have a proverb: "If you are a colonel, then your wife is a general." This was certainly the case with Lon Nol's first wife.

Cambodians believe that the wealth of a man is reflected in the jewels his wife wears at all times, even on trips to the market. For specific purposes, she may choose gold, diamonds, sapphires, rubies, or emeralds—but never silver, which is considered common. Lon Nol's wife had exquisite taste and knew exactly which jewels to wear for each purpose in order to convey the rank and social standing of her husband. She was revered throughout the country and loved by her husband, even though he had mistresses with whom he had several children. At least three of these women were known as lesser wives, and one of the three was reported to be Vietnamese, a fact I could not reconcile with the General's attitude toward these people. His mistresses lived in various sections of the city, although their children were often at the General's home.

One of the General's aides told me that an oracle once predicted that as long as the General's wife lived, everything would go well for him, but once she died, things would be different. When her death occurred in 1969, Lon Nol feared this indicated the beginning of his own decline. I often observed him grieving after her death and asking aloud what fate had in store for him. Soon, however, he surprised many of us by marrying again. This second wife was a much younger woman who was never fully accepted by the public. She preferred wearing silver jewelry, something that his first wife never would have done. In addition, I was concerned about the closed circle that formed between her and the General's younger brother Lon Non and his wife, who both lived in the residence. The three of them often appeared to be conspiring in private.

****

Despite the size of the residence, there was no quiet area where I could be alone. Within the quarters reserved for the General's aides, most of the men were boisterous and spent much of their time gambling or visiting brothels. They often enjoyed these pursuits in the company of the General's brother. After my years in the silence and austerity of the monastery, I found it hard to adjust to life among these people. Because we were not far from the large monastery in the Tuol Kauk neighborhood northwest of the city, I rose each day before dawn and walked there to join the monks in their chanting and prayers. Visiting this sacred place each morning made me feel more at home than I ever could be in the intimidating residence of General Lon Nol.

My morning ritual also provided an opportunity to make my first friend after leaving Battambang. Marcel Blanchette, from Canada, also came to the Tuol Kauk monastery each day to participate in the chants. I was surprised to see a Westerner in this place, especially one who spoke our language and knew the Buddhist chants. Because we usually walked back in the same direction after the service, we began talking together and soon discovered we each liked to start the day with the traditional Cambodian breakfast soup known as *kuy teav*. Nearby was a street vendor who had set up his large steaming pot next to a table with a few stools for sitting.

This soup consists primarily of thin square-shaped noodles cooked in boiling water, strained, placed in a large serving bowl, and moistened with more water, caramelized garlic oil, and a sticky liquid made from oyster sauce, a pinch of sugar, and soy sauce. I often watched my mother making this delicious soup. Because of our proximity to the Tonle Sap Lake, she usually included fish or shrimp in the recipe. Some people add *tik trey*, or fish sauce, but my mother did not use this in noodle dishes. In Phnom Penh, the soup usually has pieces of pork or chicken, rather than fish. The condiments, placed in small bowls on the table, may include limes, pepper from Kampot, lettuce leaves, bean sprouts, scallions, more garlic oil, fresh or dried chili peppers, and chili sauce that one can add to the soup or use as a dipping sauce for the meat.

I recall fondly the first morning that Marcel Blanchette and I enjoyed our bowls of *kuy teav*. "Narong, this soup is one of the greatest delicacies I have ever tasted—even in the best restaurants in Paris! Whenever I return to Cambodia after travels back to Quebec or to Paris, I must start the day with this soup!"

"My friend, I am not familiar with Westerners or their names. Should I address you as Marcel or Blanchette?"

"In the west, the family name comes after the given name. So please call me Marcel, rather than my family name Blanchette. It's just the opposite of Khmer names, where the given name comes last."

"Please tell me how you learned so much about my country and how you speak the language so well."

"I come from the French-Canadian province of Quebec, where most of my schooling was in the French language, as it is here in Phnom Penh. At a Jesuit-run French lycée, I learned about the adventures of early French explorers and missionaries in Cambodia and saw pictures of the majestic monuments and wild countryside with its mountains, huge waterfalls, rapids, and jungles. At that early age, I knew that I would eventually work and live in Cambodia. To prepare for this, I went to Paris to study archeology after graduating from Laval University in Quebec, where I majored in Asian history. In Paris, where I also studied the Khmer language, history, and

8

culture, I became particularly attracted to Theravada Buddhism. That is why I come to the Tuol Kauk monastery whenever I am in Phnom Penh."

"What kind work do you do, Marcel, and where?"

"I work with a team of French archeologists restoring ancient monuments in the areas of Angkor Wat and Angkor Thom. It is often difficult and dangerous, but very rewarding. Because so many of these great architectural treasures have been damaged over the centuries, we must preserve them now for future generations. Have you ever visited Angkor, Narong?"

"No. After leaving my home province of Battambang, I came directly here to serve on the staff of General Lon Nol. But one of my great dreams is to visit those sacred places that are so revered by our people."

****

In addition to getting to know Marcel Blanchette, I met many powerful people while working for the General. I knew that one of them, Prince Sisowath Sirik Matak, resented that the French had not chosen a member of his branch of the royal family as King in 1941 but instead had chosen his cousin, Prince Norodom Sihanouk. In the presence of Sirik Matak, I prostrated myself just as I would in the presence of Prince Sihanouk, since both men descended from Cambodian royalty. I believed then in the divine powers of our rulers and, by extension, all members of their families.

Over the next few years, the General announced many victories his troops had made over communist agitators in the countryside, who he said were supported and trained by the North Vietnamese to overthrow Prince Sihanouk. One of the General's aides told me that the leader of a rural branch of the Khmer communist movement had defected in return for protection, and General Lon Nol rewarded him with a spacious villa and grounds near the rice-growing area of Battambang. The aide also said that this mysterious man assuaged the General's concerns about communist agitators in Phnom Penh, explaining that the main communist figure in the capital was an old former monk named Tou Samouth, who seemed to have few followers, espoused moderate policies, and saw Sihanouk as a figure of national unity.

At the same time, Lon Nol noted that leftist students and journalists in Phnom Penh would have to be watched closely. He instructed his circle of aides and advisors to be vigilant in monitoring the activities of all students recently returned from Paris. He assigned his brother Lon Non, who commanded a special unit of police and enjoyed the support of gangs of rowdy young thugs, to follow these people closely.

The General pointed out that he had intentionally omitted two names from this list of Paris-educated students: sisters Ieng Thirith and Khieu Ponnary, who belonged to a family that had long enjoyed close ties to the royal family. He explained that Khieu Ponnary, who lived with her young husband in a house near the royal palace, was editor of Prince Sihanouk's official magazine, *Kambuja*. Her husband, Saloth Sar, served in the royal household as a boy and had been a close friend of the General's brother Lon Non when the two attended the same secondary school in Kampong Cham. The General said that there was no need to monitor the movements of these people.

One young man the police did follow closely was Khieu Samphan, who published a left-wing French language newspaper in which he criticized government policies, especially the violence shown to perceived enemies, which Samphan found incompatible with Buddhist thought. These latter sentiments actually made me admire this brave young man.

****

Out of fear that Vietnam, which seemed to be winning the war with the Americans, might try again to invade Cambodia, Sihanouk—without consulting Lon Nol—decided to sever ties with the United States, which for years had provided vital military assistance to Cambodia.

When they learned of this decision, angry pro-American members of the military and National Assembly, accompanied by Prince Sirik Matak, paid frequent visits to the General regarding Sihanouk's surprise decision. Some of these men actually raised the possibility of deposing Sihanouk, but the General's absolute loyalty to the prince never wavered.

After several such exchanges, Sirik Matak left abruptly, with an angry and exasperated look on his face. These emotional meetings took a toll on the General, who suffered from the dilemma of remaining loyal to Sihanouk, while at the same time recognizing how the Prince's policies were straining the military. Without American military assistance, government forces would never be able to counter a Vietnamese attack. Trying to deal with this dangerous situation, the General frequently broke down in tears and began spending more time in private praying with the nine monks who lived at the residence.

The General's circle of holy men upon whom he relied for advice soon expanded to ten. The General received a message from his senior officer in Kampong Thom regarding a Buddhist monk from a remote northeastern province who was considered a visionary and performed miracles. This monk also proclaimed himself the reincarnation of Jayavarman VII. Word was spreading throughout the country about this holy man, who also claimed that the Buddha had pre-ordained Lon Nol to restore the Khmer nation to its former glory.

After ordering his commanders to find the exact location of the holy man, the General appointed a small group consisting of two of his Buddhist advisors and two armed soldiers on a quest to bring him to Phnom Penh. I was thrilled when the General asked me to accompany them. Because there were no roads connecting the capital to the mountains of the northeast, we had to make the grueling trip on foot to bring the holy man to Phnom Penh.

Once we began the journey into the mountainous terrain of the north, we were struck by the poverty of the people living in that region. We saw men and women who were only in their thirties or forties but looked to be twice that age, trying to grow crops in land never affected by the beneficial seasonal floods that occurred in other parts of the country. Rice and fish, the two main staples of our diet, were unheard of there because there was no easy access to the more prosperous areas of the country. Anyone traveling to that wild region from Phnom Penh usually had to go into Vietnam and re-enter Cambodia from the east. Now, however, the fighting in Vietnam prevented us from taking that route.

Fortunately, one of the monks in our company came from the northeastern region and could identify paths through the jungles and arduous mountain passages. Along the way, one of the two soldiers in our group contracted malaria and began shaking so violently that he could no longer walk. He also lost all of his hair and fell into a coma. We created a type of stretcher that enabled us to carry the poor man until we reached a temple where the monks promised to care for him. On our return, we discovered that the soldier had died because of the lack of medicine in that remote area.

After several grueling days of walking without much nourishment in the hot and humid forests and jungles, we found the holy man named Mam Prum Mony. Once he learned that Lon Nol had sent us, he responded enthusiastically to our invitation to accompany us to Phnom Penh. In fact, it seemed as if he already knew why we had come. As we traveled back to Phnom Penh, he helped us to identify plants of medicinal value and to find edible roots, insects, and snails. He also showed us how to make infusions of tea from the bark and leaves of wild plants.

Mam Prum Mony would eventually prove to be invaluable when Lon Nol's loyalty to Prince Sihanouk was put to the test. Over the years, this man, who added to his name the title of Great Intellectual of Pure Glory, would become Lon Nol's most important spiritual and political advisor. Nevertheless, I eventually came to doubt many of his claims and believe he took advantage of the General's gullible nature.

In November 1965, Prince Sihanouk summoned the General to his residence and asked him to undertake a mission that must have been difficult for him to accept. This assignment was part of a diplomatic campaign to ensure Cambodia's neutrality and the preservation of its borders while the Americans were waging war in Vietnam. The Prince explained to Lon Nol that he needed to work with communist leaders in China, Laos, and Vietnam in order to seek the Middle Way espoused by the Buddha. Lon Nol was to begin this process during a visit to

China. While we on the staff were unaware of this, Sihanouk asked Lon Nol to sign a treaty allowing China to ship arms and other supplies from southwestern Cambodian ports to the Ho Chi Minh trail in the northeast, for onward shipment to North Vietnamese troops. Sihanouk also wanted Lon Nol's army to ensure safe passage of this material through Cambodian territory.

When the General returned from his meeting with the Prince, he was shaking. After a few minutes, he was calm enough to go back to his office, accompanied by Mam Prum Moni, who began chanting in a low voice. For a man who hated the Vietnamese, accepting this new mission from Prince Sihanouk must have been one of the most trying moments of the General's life.

I tried to look into his office to see what was happening. Although the blinds on all the windows were shut, a ray of light on one side of the room created a shadow on the opposite wall. As the chanting ended, I could make out the shadow of the holy man standing over the prostrate General. The holy man's voice sounded distant and much deeper than usual. As strange, unearthly sounds came from his mouth, the voice identified itself as that of Jayavarman VII. The General's body trembled before the holy man through whom the great king of Angkor was speaking. The voice proclaimed:

> You, Lon Nol of Chenla, are like Rama, the hero of the epic portrayed on the walls of Angkor Wat. Like you, Rama was not a god, but merely a mortal who faced fearsome, unnerving dilemmas. Like you, he overcame these by following what we Buddhists call the *dharma,* the righteous way. You, Lon Nol of Chenla, will find that righteous path even if it takes you to lands that you fear, among people that you hate.
>
> You have been divinely chosen by the Buddha himself to protect the rulers of our nation. Until you come into your own as ruler of the Khmer people, your duty is to support and protect my descendants on the royal throne of the kings of Angkor. As the ancient warriors depicted on the walls of Angkor Wat entered

the sea of churning milk and drank of the nectar of immortality, so you, Lon Nol of Chenla, will be invincible and protected from evil as you follow the righteous path toward the glorious destiny that awaits you.

As the otherworldly voice died away and his own voice returned, Mam Prum Mony ordered the General to stand. The holy man, who had the power to prepare magic potions and charms, pinned onto the General's uniform a special piece of cloth that would aid him through these difficult times. When the General turned toward me and the aides and monks waiting outside the room, he seemed like a changed man. He smiled and walked resolutely toward his private rooms to prepare for the trip to China.

After the tragic events of 1975, Lon Nol remembered with great pride the fact that the voice of Jayavarman VII chose to address him as "Lon Nol of Chenla." When the kingdom of Chenla conquered the Funan kingdom to its south, the powerful Khmer dynasty began. For this reason, Lon Nol's two major military operations were called Chenla 1 and Chenla 2.

****

Because of my experience in the monastery studying the teachings of the Buddha, I began to see Lon Nol as typical of those who seek to achieve enlightenment but do not have the fortitude to persevere. The Buddha teaches that humans are limited by what we call *samsara,* or the endless cycle of birth, aging, illness, death, and rebirth. To escape from this wearisome cycle, one must follow the Four Noble Truths: *"Suffering exists. Suffering is caused by craving or desire. Release from suffering can be achieved by stopping all craving or desire. Enlightenment can be achieved by following the Noble Eight-Fold Path."* The eight steps along that path are *right views, right intention, right speech, right action, right livelihood, right effort, right mindfulness, and right concentration.* It is only by complying with these rules of moral conduct that a person can improve his *karma,* or chances of happiness in this life and the next. The monks surrounding the General repeatedly stressed these precepts, as well as the five basic commandments for right living: *Do not kill. Do not steal. Do not indulge in forbidden sexual pleasures. Do not tell lies. Do not take intoxicants, stupefying drugs, or alcohol.*

Despite having spent hours with the monks and holy men around him, General Lon Nol lacked the resolve to take to heart the precepts of the Four Noble Truths and sincerely apply them to his own actions. He was also too gullible, believing every claim made by Mam Prum Mony, trusting that the holy man could provide him with easy solutions to his problems. Like others who lack the concentration and effort to achieve enlightenment, the General too often seemed to fall into an aimless existence in which he was happy one moment but in despair the next.

****

The next year was marked by developments that, viewed from today's perspective, led inevitably to Sihanouk's demise and to Lon Nol's triumph, as well as great shame. To solve the nation's grave economic crisis, Sihanouk opened several casinos in the hope that it would save the country from bankruptcy. While Lon Nol and others, including Queen Mother Kossamak, made enormous profits from this scheme, many ordinary people lost their homes and savings, while others committed suicide.

To assuage the concerns of the military and others, the Prince created what he termed a Salvation Government, with Lon Nol as Prime Minister and Sirik Matak as Deputy Prime Minister. During that time, the two men engaged in lengthy discussions at the residence. From what I could hear, it appeared that both men had at last agreed upon the need for a change in government, although Sirik Matak was in favor of removing Sihanouk completely, while Lon Nol favored a constitutional amendment allowing the prince to remain as a figurehead.

A year later, in March 1970, the Prince was planning to return home from his annual dietary cure in France. Suddenly, however, he sent a telegram to Queen Mother Kossamak, telling her that he had changed his plans and decided to go ahead with a previously planned visit to Moscow and Beijing en route to home. Upon hearing of this, Sirik Matak rushed to the General's office. The whole staff could hear him shouting, "It is time now to get rid of Sihanouk! By going to Moscow and Beijing, it is obvious that he has sold out to the communists! If Sihanouk is out of the picture, I know the Americans will give us their full economic and military support! These actions by Sihanouk should finally convince you to forget your loyalty and allegiance to this man who has become a traitor to the Khmer people!"

"This is a painful decision for me, old friend," replied Lon Nol. "An oracle told me I would one day rule over our great country, and I see now that my time has come. I am ready!"

The two men made a visit to the Queen Mother to inform her of their intentions. Shortly after that visit, a story began circulating throughout the city that the Queen summoned a senior *baku,* one of the royal court's Hindu Brahman priests, to preside over a secret ceremony to see if her son would return to power. The *baku* reportedly handed her a sacred sword from its scabbard. As she removed it, she withdrew in horror as she saw that it had turned a hideous black color. She believed this represented the worst possible omen for her son. Whether this event actually occurred, or someone close to Lon Nol planted an expedient story, will probably never be known.

Rumors quickly began circulating around the capital that Sihanouk had betrayed his people and was now collaborating with the Chinese, Russian, and Vietnamese communists. Sihanouk never did return to Cambodia but remained in Beijing as a guest of the Chinese government. As a result, when the bloodless coup occurred on March 20, most people in the city rejoiced. They were tired of the Prince's obsession with filmmaking and of the overwhelming economic crisis that was affecting people at all levels of society.

Once Sihanouk was deposed, it was not his aristocratic cousin Sirik Matak who replaced him, but the peasant-like Lon Nol. "Milord Daddy" had been replaced by "Black Papa." The

Buddha had chosen this flawed man over the descendants of the royal families to become leader of the Khmer people.

The General believed that the Buddha had chosen him to save our land from the Vietnamese infidels and return us once more to the glorious days of Angkor. Lon Nol had reason to be proud of what he had accomplished, but his initial euphoria quickly faded. Once the coup succeeded, the General realized the enormity of what he had set into motion. He rushed to the palace and prostrated himself at the feet of the Queen Mother, begging her forgiveness for what he had done.

Shortly after his visit to the Queen Mother, Lon Nol made a radio address to the nation. He began with these words: "An oracle predicted that all Cambodians will one day enjoy equal rights, that the bad king will flee, and Cambodia will become a republic." He explained that the predictions of this oracle had now come to pass and that a new day had begun. He proclaimed this new day as the official end of the centuries-old Cambodian monarchy.

While most residents of Phnom Penh were relieved to see the end of Sihanouk's reign, Lon Nol's announcement was not welcomed by peasants still living under a feudal system where all good came from the god-king. My mother wrote to me from Battambang that peasants began asking, "How shall we tend our rice paddies, now that the King is not here to make it rain?"

In the weeks and months following the coup, several senior American officials came to Phnom Penh to assess the situation and meet with Lon Nol, who believed that the Americans intended to send large numbers of troops and advisors into Cambodia now that their war with Vietnam was over. He did not realize that the Americans had no desire to get involved in another military conflict in the region.

One of the first senior U.S. officials to visit Lon Nol was General Alexander Haig. Lon Nol told the American general, "My small country is not equipped to resist any large-scale Vietnamese attacks. My troops need the type of training and other military support that your more experienced American soldiers can provide. Now that your troops are preparing to leave Vietnam, it should be easy for your soldiers to join us in our fight against the Vietnamese communists."

"While I sympathize with your situation, the United States can provide only limited support. Because Congress has voted not to authorize our sending troops to Cambodia, we can offer very restricted economic and military aid."

After his meeting with the American general, Lon Nol emerged shaking, with tears pouring from his eyes. For over an hour after the American left, I could hear the General weeping alone in his office and calling out the name of his deceased first wife.

****

Lon Nol's hopes revived after the receipt of a letter from the man whose letters to Lon Nol would continue until August 1974, and in whom the General placed complete confidence. This man, who promised needed assistance and encouragement, was Richard M. Nixon, President of the United States of America. Years later, when I was with the General in exile in Hawaii, he handed me a leather portfolio containing the entire correspondence between him and the American president. He was fearful of leaving the letters in the hands of his second wife, whom he had grown to distrust.

Throughout the years, I have kept these letters in safe places. Before recording my life story to share with others, however, I needed to know more about the contents of this correspondence. Lon Nol's letters were written in French, as were President Nixon's letters to Lon Nol (after translation in Washington). Like most of my countrymen, I could understand some spoken French but never learned the written language. I therefore sought the assistance of my friend, Marcel Blanchette, who had returned to Cambodia in the 1990s with his team of French archeologists.

Marcel was the most trustworthy and competent person I knew to handle this translation. Fluent in French, English, and Khmer, my Canadian friend understood and could explain to me American attitudes and culture. He gladly offered to work with me in deciphering the content of the letters. For over one month in late 2013, we spent long evenings together about three or four times a week so that I could write down the words Marcel was translating into Khmer.

President Nixon's first letter, dated 7 April 1970, was obviously not what the General had hoped to hear, especially in light of reassurances from American emissaries that their president would find a way to help Cambodia despite restrictions placed on him by Congress. Sadly, Lon Nol should have seen that first letter as proof of what one observer later concluded; namely, that the Americans viewed Cambodia merely as a "sideshow," while the main event was going on elsewhere. The opening lines of the first letter moved Lon Nol to tears. It read:

Dear Mr. Prime Minister,

I have viewed with concern the continuing deterioration of the situation in Laos. I ask you, as a neighbor of Laos and one who is no doubt concerned about the situation in that war-torn country, to share your thoughts as to how one might help to bring about peace in Laos.

President Nixon's letter made no mention of the plight of Cambodia. Lon Nol agonized for days over how to respond to this letter. He called upon Sirik Matak, Mam Prum Mony, and others to determine how best to make the case for Cambodia in this first message to the American president. Once he had finished the letter, he decided that he needed his own official seal to replace the seal of the royal family used by Sihanouk. The new seal portrayed a seated Buddha surrounded by magical symbols designed by Mam Prum Mony. In his response, dated 14 April 1970, Lon Nol assured President Nixon:

My government will support international diplomatic efforts to ensure the neutrality of Laos. But, while I agree that the situation in Laos is serious, I want you to understand the equally alarming nature of the situation in Cambodia and the grave danger which menaces all countries of Indochina.

When no response had yet arrived from Washington, the General sent a more detailed letter a week later to the American president, stating the following:

Cambodia is presently a victim of open aggression by the VC and NVA [the Viet Cong and North Vietnamese Army] with the complicity of the former Chief of State, Prince Norodom Sihanouk. The VC and NVA openly and daily attack our defense forces and our villages in flagrant violation of the U.N. charter, international law, and of the Geneva accords of 1964.

The Government which I head has the total support of the army, of the youth, of the clergy, and of all social levels of the population; but we lack arms, materials, military equipment, and munitions with which to organize ourselves. We also lack aircraft and helicopters. I have the honor to call upon Your Excellency to help us in these tragic circumstances.

While transcribing these words, I told Marcel, "I realize now that these carefully chosen words may not have been fully understood by the American president. Because Lon Nol saw the conflict in Cambodia in part as a holy war to preserve Buddhism, he believed it important to underline the support he enjoyed from the clergy."

"Yes, my friend. You knew how troubled Lon Nol was by the large number of young people defecting from the government. You also understood his desire to show President Nixon that he could count on the support of the young as well.

"Have you noticed that in none of the letters to President Nixon did Lon Nol state that those threatening his regime were fellow Cambodians? Rather, he always described the enemy as the North and South Vietnamese or Laotian communists. I'm sure he believed that by doing this, he would get a better response from the Americans."

"I agree, Marcel. Lon Nol hesitated to admit to anyone, including the American president, that he was fighting against fellow ethnic Khmers. He hated the Vietnamese and believed the Khmers were a superior race. He truly believed he would one day return his country to the glory it enjoyed under the kings of Angkor."

****

While waiting for promised American assistance, and as attacks against the Cambodian army increased throughout the country, Lon Nol sent letters to his division commanders, instructing them to tell their troops to rely on magic and the power of spirits, as had their ancestors. Along with these letters, he sent boxes with pieces of cloth bearing the words "Mam Prum Mony, Great Intellectual of Pure Glory." The General instructed officers to tell their troops that these cloths blessed by the holy man would protect them if they stepped on mines or were the targets of bullets or shrapnel.

At the holy man's request, the General also had special plants placed in a garden near Pochentong Airport outside of Phnom Penh. He told his officers that wearing a small piece of the plant's root, or drinking it in a concoction with brandy or other spirits before battle, would protect their troops from harm. To protect the city from attack, Mam Prum Mony gave the General some sand he had blessed, claiming it had special magic. Lon Nol dutifully ordered helicopter pilots to spread this sand around the perimeter of Phnom Penh, following the ritual boundaries of the pagodas circling the city, in order to create a "sacred enclosure" for the capital.

At about this same time, President Nixon sent Lon Nol an object that the General revered as a talisman with special powers: a fountain pen bearing the seal of the Presidency. Upon receipt of this gift, the General had a carved teak box created, with a gold-inlaid slot to hold the pen. On top of the ornate box, the General placed a gold-framed photo of Richard Nixon that he had found in a magazine.

I felt pity for the General, who placed such importance on this small gift and did not question why the American president would not have selected a more important tribute to this man who worshipped him. In a letter dated 9 June 1970, the General spoke of the "emotion and joy" with which he received the pen. He added:

> I was much touched with this attention on your part and that you had this kind thought despite the many problems which beset you. I much admire this very handsome object and I will conserve it as a souvenir of the generous and far-sighted President who has not hesitated to come to the assistance of my country. I hope to be able to make use of it for the signing of documents which will later be considered as decisive steps in the history of the struggles of the people and for true democracy.

Nixon, in response, thanked him for his "exceedingly kind words regarding the fountain pen." As it turned out, Lon Nol never had the occasion to use the pen for his stated purpose. There never were any official agreements or documents exchanged between the two countries, nor any meaningful communication between Lon Nol and the U.S. Government. Lon Nol and Sirik Matak trusted the Americans completely, and Lon Nol considered President Nixon a friend on whom he could always rely.

Less than a month after the first exchange of letters between Lon Nol and President Nixon, we began to see deliveries of military equipment and economic assistance from the Americans. One of President Nixon's letters stated:

> I assure you that my government will take what measures it can effectively take to assist you in facing Viet Cong and North Vietnamese violation of Cambodian territory. I understand and sympathize with your deep concern in this regard.

In the coming months, the United States moved their bombing missions deeper into Khmer territory. Despite reports from field commanders that such operations were counter-productive and actually driving peasants to join the Khmer

Rouge, the General ignored the reports and kept asking for more and more bombing missions.

In return for U.S. equipment and money, Lon Nol promised the American president that he would undertake the rebuilding of the Khmer Army from about 35,000 poorly trained, ill-equipped men into an effective fighting force of 110,000. To accomplish this formidable task, the General sent out trucks to collect young men in places where they usually congregated, such as cinemas and cafés. Naive and unprepared young men received cursory drills in open spaces and were sent directly into battle. Although large numbers either died in the first minutes of battle or defected once they had their first taste of battle, Lon Nol kept these losses hidden from the public. At the same time, commanders often kept the names of these soldiers on their rolls and continued to receive payments from the Americans for what were actually "phantom" troops.

Despite increased American bombing missions, combined North Vietnamese and Khmer Rouge forces moved deeper into Cambodian territory. In June 1970, only three months after the coup, Vietnamese communist forces succeeded in taking control of Angkor Wat, the traditional source of pride to the Khmer people. This audacious act stunned Lon Nol, who went into a period of depression and begged Mam Prum Mony to restore his spirits. Upon the holy man's advice, I went to the Central Market (*Phsar Thmei*) where the Chinese doctor's daughter, who treated those suffering from emotional troubles, prepared mixtures of herbs and other plant materials to be put into infusions for the General. These seemed to appease the General's anxiety.

About this same time, the General began a series of consultations with one of his long-time associates and friends, a military officer named Um Savuth, who was a member of the ethnic Muslim group in Cambodia known as the Chams. These consultations did not take place in the General's residence, but rather during rides in a jeep driven by General Savuth at notoriously dangerous speeds. Lon Nol enjoyed these rides tremendously, and they seemed to do more than the herbal mixtures to assuage his tortured soul.

General Savuth descended from the famed warriors of the Kingdom of Champa, which once ruled most of central and southern Vietnam and eastern parts of Cambodia. In the twelfth century, the Khmers had lost much of Angkor to these Muslim people, but Jayavarman VII ultimately defeated the invading Chams. Despite the wars between the two groups, Khmer and Cham engaged in profitable trade relations for many centuries. The royal families of both cultures intermarried frequently, and the Chams even adopted some of the religious beliefs and superstitious practices of the Khmer people, while at the same time adhering to their own belief in Islam. The Chams, whose main population center was the Mekong Delta area known to Cambodians as Kampuchea Krom, also established important centers in Kampong Chhnang, Battambang, and Phnom Penh.

Like the General, I admired the Cham people of Cambodia. Many of them lived in houseboats along the rivers and became successful fishermen. Others made beautiful textiles of exquisite design. I often admired the silks and other beautiful cloths sold by the Chams whenever I visited the Central Market in Phnom Penh. As the Khmer Rouge gradually destroyed most of the silk-making industry, only one silk merchant remained at the Central Market: a Cham woman, a descendent of those enterprising people who for centuries represented an important link on the Silk Road from the Middle East to China.

As a young monk in Battambang, I loved to visit the Cham villages whose residents responded generously to our requests for alms and rice for the poor. These villages were set apart and often designed in a circular formation, at the center of which was a mosque. The men usually had beards and wore small round caps on their heads, while the priests, known as *mufti*, wore turbans. The women, with their long, colorful scarves, were said to have elaborate hairstyles. Cham women also wore beautiful jewels and were believed to possess magical powers. Cham men were considered the fiercest fighters in Cambodia.

Cham General Um Savuth was considered a brave, although sometimes reckless, commander. As a young officer, he once asked a subordinate to place a cat on his head and then ordered the young man to move several paces away and shoot at the cat.

The soldier missed the cat; the bullet blew away part of Savuth's brain, leaving him paralyzed on one side. He was a thin man whose body leaned to one side, necessitating a long white cane to steady himself. Drinking too much also contributed to his unsteady gait; in fact, Savuth was usually drunk when he drove Lon Nol off at precariously high speeds to discuss how to respond to the Vietnamese invasion of Angkor Wat.

While the two men were formulating an offensive to reopen the road to Kampong Thom and remove the Vietnamese from Angkor, Lon Nol failed to consult either the General Staff or Army Chief. These more competent military officers, appalled at Lon Nol's bypassing their input and at his choice of commander for this important mission, were prevented from expressing their fears and outrage directly to Lon Nol, who refused to hear criticism of any sort. Lon Nol referred to this, his first major military operation, as Chenla I.

In August 1970, a long thin line of unskilled and untrained troops, with their families straggling behind, deployed along a narrow stretch of the road leading to Kampong Thom, part of which consisted of raised causeways between the flooded rice paddies. This weak, extended line of frightened raw recruits proved to be an easy target for combined North Vietnamese, Viet Cong, and Khmer Rouge units who slaughtered thousands of troops, destroyed bridges faster than the army could rebuild them, and killed many of the families attempting to flee from the carnage. Lon Nol took advantage of the traditionally bad lines of communication between Phnom Penh and the provinces, and declared victory over the invading enemy forces. Large celebrations were held throughout the capital as people hailed Lon Nol as the conquering hero of Chenla I.

President Nixon wrote to Lon Nol:

> It was with the greatest pleasure that I read your assessment of the dynamic forces your country [brought to bear] against communist aggression. The strong and effective defense already presented by the Cambodian armed forces has inspired my own admiration and that of the American people. The United States intends to continue to provide support for your country in its brave

and determined struggle. I am confident that the Cambodian sense of nationalism and liberty, which you so eloquently described, will prevail.

For the next few months, Lon Nol basked in an outpouring of popular support and grew more confident in his hopes of realizing his dream of winning what he perceived as a holy war that would lead to the creation of a new nation to rival that of the ancient kings of Angkor. At the end of 1970, he sent New Year's greetings to President Nixon, thanking him for his assistance and assuring him:

> The Khmers are succeeding in tipping the scales. It is now the North Vietnamese, South Vietnamese, and Laotian communists who are the ones under attack. I have high praise for the U.S. bombing missions along the Ho Chi Minh trail and into the provinces of Kampong Thom, Kratie, and Kampong Cham. In addition, our own planes will make every effort to destroy any remaining enemy troops.

Lon Nol's euphoria was short-lived. On 21 January 1971, North Vietnamese units attacked Pochentong Airport outside the capital and destroyed all of the Khmer Air Force planes, including its Russian MIG fighter jets. Residents of Phnom Penh now saw the alleged victory of Chenla I for what it was: a lie and an illusion. The public mood quickly changed from shock to dismay, and lastly, to anger. Soon, people began calling for Lon Nol's ouster. On 4 February 1971, Lon Nol suffered a debilitating stroke and flew to an American medical facility in Hawaii for treatment.

****

At the time of the General's stroke, I had served with him for twelve years and did not know if I would ever see him again. His scheming brother Lon Non and his wife, along with the General's second wife, made it clear to the General's staff aides and holy men that they were no longer welcome. Lon Non allowed us to remain at the residence in case the General did recover and return to Phnom Penh, but we could no longer enter the General's office. At about the same time, I received word that my mother's health was deteriorating, and I decided to go to her at once. Although two of the General's bodyguards who were going to Battambang at that time offered to take me with them, I wanted to make this journey of 275 kilometers (over 170 miles) by myself.

I was now almost thirty years old, approximately the same age as the Buddha when he left his princely home in India to meet his subjects. Leaving behind his life of privilege, he became a mendicant; several years later, while sitting under a *bodhi* tree, he attained enlightenment. As soon as I left the city of Phnom Penh, I felt that I too was on a journey toward some type of awakening or enlightenment. Several times during my two-week journey, kindly people invited me to join them in their donkey carts, thus sparing my feet and giving me a chance to rest a bit.

One day as I was walking toward my destination, I recalled the legend that the Buddha and his cousin Ananda once traveled through ancient Cambodia on foot. On one particularly hot day, they stopped in the shade of a *thlok* tree for their noon meal, which consisted of food from the heavens. As I came upon one of these trees, whose kiwi-like fruit has often fed our people in times of famine, I sat under its shade and prayed to the Buddha.

The farther I walked, the more rural the landscape became, and the more I felt truly at home. I followed the Tonle Sap River northward up to where it met the Tonle Sap Lake, continuing along the western edge of the lake toward Battambang. It was easy to make my way along the river because it was still the dry season. Once the monsoon rains came in May, the roads would disappear while the lake would grow in size from twelve hundred square miles to over three thousand square miles. Periodically I stopped to talk with residents of floating villages who welcomed me and shared their meals of perch, smelt, or carp, accompanied by delicious fruits such as the mangosteen, mango, or durian.

Unlike my days as a young monk when I was penniless, I now had money to pay these people for their hospitality. Nonetheless, most villagers refused any offers of money. Instead, they gathered friends and family in the evening to hear stories about the city of Phnom Penh, which most of them had never seen and which they considered too full of foreigners. They also told me of their fear of attacks by the Vietnamese. Although they did not say much about "the others" who had joined the Khmer Rouge, I could sense some affection on their part for these people, especially now that Prince Sihanouk had allied himself with the Khmer Rouge. Peasants and villagers still referred to the Prince as *Samdech Euv* and usually had pictures of him in their homes. A few years later, the Khmer Rouge would kill people merely for having pictures of the Prince on their walls.

I envied people who made their living along the river and lakes, and the beauty and rhythm of their lives continue to inspire me. I marveled at the gracefulness of fishermen in their narrow flat-bottomed boats, standing precariously at one end and bending their bodies forward while holding onto one oar to move their boats along. Later they would stop to throw their nets into the fish-laden water. The soft splashing of the nets hitting the water served to bring back memories of my childhood. Several times along my journey, I dove into the water where I loved to swim as a young boy. On these hot days toward the end of the dry season, this kept my body refreshed as I moved closer toward home.

Above the shimmering water, I could see herons searching for fish and diving straight down toward their prey. Now and then, the delicate upraised ears on the top of a white rhinoceros's head would peek out at me from the shallow water. Why such a huge, ugly creature had such delicate ears amazed me. Perhaps this unlikely configuration only serves to remind us of the interrelationships between all sentient beings and to strengthen our belief that our spirits can move from one life form to another during various incarnations. I surmised that the spirit now living in this creature could once have been an overly curious person who listened to neighbors' conversations in order to pass along gossip. Now it could only listen without sharing with others whatever bits of news it overheard along the river.

Moving away from the lake, I saw other sights from my childhood, including herders leading their cattle toward wooden houses built high on stilts to protect them from the monsoon floods. Once I saw the rice paddy fields stretching out beyond the horizon I knew I was close to home. As I approached my mother's house, I recognized it at once, not only by sight but also by the smell of jasmine and other fragrant vines climbing around the stilts and onto the roof. One side of her house was framed by graceful tall palm fronds and a small Star Fruit tree (*Taloeung Toeung*) with dark pink flower petals and bright yellow fruit. In front of her house was a small pond where, as a boy, I loved to watch the dragonflies gliding over the lotus blossoms.

I climbed the steep wooden steps and entered the one room where we had lived, ate, and slept when I was a young boy. Here I saw my mother lying on a cot, surrounded by some of her elderly friends who came each day to feed and comfort her. Each woman rose to greet me with palms joined together and raised toward the forehead in the traditional Cambodian manner, while I moved onto my knees to kiss my mother's moist cheek. When the other women left, my mother and I talked only briefly because I could see that she tired easily. After a few days, her spirits seemed revived by my presence. I spoke of my love for this part of the countryside and my desire to remain here. While I did not tell her of my doubts about the General and my concerns about remaining with him, she sensed my unease.

"I know you are concerned about going back to Phnom Penh, my son, but you must return. It is a matter of respect for Lon Nol's wife, who arranged for you to work for her husband. If you break this bond of honor I have with her, I fear it would create bad *karma* for me now that I am ready to leave this life for the next. Please do not stay here, my son."

"I understand, *Makk*. The General's wife was very kind to me. I promise you, *Makk*, that I will not dishonor the bond you have made. After my visit here, I will go back to Phnom Penh."

I kissed her and held her hand as she drifted off to sleep. I knew that my mother's health was quickly deteriorating and that she would not live to see the monsoon rains.

During the last few nights, her friends came to the house to share stories and folk tales. One night, when a full moon shone down on the glistening pond in front of the house, the women recounted the legend that the shadows on the face of the moon were those of a *bodhi* tree, in whose shade sits an old woman working at her loom, weaving silk cloth for the people on earth.

That night, as I slept on the cot next to that of my mother, I had a wonderful dream. I was a young boy again, walking toward the rice paddies. A shadow suddenly fell over the field, and clouds of migrating orange butterflies, covering many miles, floated above the paddies and lotus-filled waters. As I gazed toward the sky, it was through the prism of thousands of fluttering orange wings. In my dream, the butterflies dipped down toward the ground where they alighted on branches and leaves of trees. I could feel something soft enveloping my body and looked down to see that my entire body was covered with thousands of pulsating orange butterflies.

At the end of the dream, I saw the old woman at her loom on the face of the moon. She was handing me a long piece of cloth of the same orange color as the wings of the butterflies. It was made not of silk, but of the simple cloth worn by Buddhist monks. This dream, the night before my mother's death, reassured me that I would once again wear the orange robe of a monk. It sustained me for many more years, until I made the final solemn vows as a Buddhist monk and returned once more to the land of my boyhood and my dreams.

After my mother's death, her elderly friends and other villagers accompanied me to the nearby temple where her body was cremated and her ashes placed in the *stupa* that housed the ashes of other family members. The night before my return to Phnom Penh, there was no reassuring dream. Instead, I was disturbed by a terrible nightmare in which I was walking through the paddy fields when suddenly a dark cloud blocked out the sun. Unlike the shimmering cloud of orange butterflies I had seen in my earlier dream, thousands of black crows now filled the sky, swooping down like herons diving for fish. The vicious, screaming black crows attacked men, women, and children, tearing at their flesh and gouging out their eyes. Once they had destroyed everything in their path, the black cloud of shrieking crows with blood dripping from their beaks moved on. As I looked down at the pond in front of me, the lotus flowers and dragonflies were gone, and the water had changed to blood.

I now know this was a premonition of the devastation to befall my country and its people, devastation instigated by those later referred to as Black Crows (*Ka-ek Khmao* in Khmer) because of the black clothes they wore and their fierce, glowering facial expressions as they moved people out of the cities and toward the killing fields.

When I awoke the following morning, I burned three sticks of incense, raised my hands together over my head, and prayed to the Buddha for my people and my land. While the Hindus brought us their gods who inspired the monuments of Angkor Wat, it was the Buddha who changed our hearts, and to whom we must return.

****

On the day that I planned to return to Phnom Penh, a soldier arrived at my mother's house to inform me that General Lon Nol, now back from Hawaii, had arranged for one of his pilots to fly me back to the capital in a plane bringing rice and other supplies for the General's family and entourage. I was relieved and grateful for this offer since I knew that the monsoon season was starting and that many of roads southward would be flooded. Besides, I lacked the energy that had characterized the earlier trip to see my mother and relive the memories of my childhood. Despite the heat and distance, that journey on foot had refreshed and enlightened me in ways I had not anticipated. I did not look forward to the trip back to Phnom Penh, knowing that it would be filled not just with sadness at leaving my home village but also with dread and anxiety.

I had never flown in a plane before and marveled at this privileged view of the land from the perspective of the birds.

Because I was the only passenger in the small plane, the pilot allowed me to sit in front with him. After a short while in the air, I looked toward the east where I could see many objects falling from a large plane. Although it actually happened much faster, the objects are always dropping in slow motion, as in a film, in my memories of that day. Once the objects landed, I could see puffs of dust rising up from the earth, just as water spouts upward like a fountain once a stone is tossed into it. Similarly, as concentric circles of waves spread out from the location where a stone falls into the water, larger circles of dust spread outward from the places on the ground where the hard objects landed. I asked the pilot to explain what we had just seen.

"Those objects are bombs aimed at Vietnamese targets on the ground. Once they land, they pulverize the targets, leaving nothing untouched."

"What kind of targets are they aiming at?" The pilot did not or could not answer.

****

I was astonished to learn about these attacks and wondered what must have been pulverized into dust when the bombs fell from the sky. Did farmers, peasants, monks, animals, insects, and birds escape from these bombs? Did they have time to flee before the bombs landed? What did it sound like down at their level? Were they all destroyed along with the enemy targets?

Once back at the General's residence, I learned that the Americans had increased their B-52 bombing raids. Even in Phnom Penh, we would hear the terrible sounds and feel the reverberations caused by those bombs as they landed in areas surrounding the city. I heard many reports of the devastation caused by the bombing campaign as more and more people sought refuge in Phnom Penh. One such story that affected me deeply concerned a funeral procession where hundreds of peasants were killed as they unwittingly marched into the B-52 target zone.

The city was filled with rumors of an impending coup, perhaps by Prince Sirik Matak, whom people believed the

Americans preferred over Lon Nol. But Sirik Matak had earlier renounced his royal title, denied any personal ambitions, and proclaimed his loyalty to Lon Nol. Nonetheless, the General's younger brother Lon Non (usually referred to as Little Brother) perceived Sirik Matak as the main threat to his own and to his brother's political viability.

Little Brother was the real person in charge during Lon Nol's absence. He commanded a military police unit of over ten thousand elite troops stationed around the capital. He could also count on the support of loud young ruffians and petty criminals, whom he referred to as "youths and intellectuals," to quell any disturbances or anti-government demonstrations.

Whereas the General preferred to spend most of his time at his residence, Little Brother made his presence known forcefully. He regularly rode around the city in a long maroon Mercedes surrounded by trucks filled with bodyguards and preceded by two or three jeeps with loudspeakers and sirens. During his trips throughout the city, he often wore a uniform made of camouflage material designed and made for him in Paris.

After his return from Hawaii, Lon Nol announced his decision to resign temporarily because of partial paralysis caused by the stroke, but acting head of state Cheng Heng asked the General to remain in office and form a new government. Most people believed this reversal on Heng's part was due to pressure from Little Brother, who insisted that the colonels and troops loyal to him would accept no one but Lon Nol as their commander.

One of Lon Nol's military aides confided to me that the Americans had promised millions more dollars in military and economic aid to Cambodia and that Little Brother, who had already siphoned off millions destined for military assistance, could not allow these funds to fall into the hands of any other potential Cambodian leader. With Lon Nol still in office, Little Brother would be assured of a continued source of funds for himself, his family, and his private gangs of thugs and loyal colonels.

****

The correspondence between Lon Nol and President Nixon continued until 1974. Now that I am able to comprehend the content of those letters, I am appalled at the extent to which each man tried to deceive the other. I often wonder how different our lives would have been if each had been truthful with the other. For his part, Lon Nol continually told President Nixon of the loyalty of the Khmer people to his government and his certainty that government forces were gaining the upper hand.

In one of his letters, the American president told Lon Nol:

> I am confident that your presence serves as an inspiration to your fellow countrymen. Cambodia represents a concrete illustration of the Nixon Doctrine in which a country aided by the United States assumes primary responsibility for its own defense. Cambodia serves as an inspiration for free people around the world.

In response, Lon Nol told Nixon of his plans to increase his forces to an unrealistic 270,000 men. A week earlier, when members of the General Staff had learned of this scheme, they had sent the well-respected General Sak Sutsakhan to convince Lon Nol of the impossibility of his plan. Lon Nol had merely dismissed Sutsakhan, who left the residence in anger. I overheard General Sutsakhan telling an aide that the idea of creating a force of that size was just another of "Lon Nol's fairyland ambitions."

Using language less cynical than that of Sak Sutsakhan, President Nixon replied diplomatically:

> After a careful study of your proposal to increase your armed forces to a level of 270,000 men, this is not a realistic proportion in terms of the training and logistics resources currently available.

By August 1971, Lon Nol announced that he planned to undertake a second major military offensive to reopen Route 6 to relieve a yearlong siege of Kampong Thom resulting from the tragic Chenla I campaign. He called this new venture Chenla II. Um Savuth, in charge of the Chenla I disaster, was replaced by another general as overall commander of this second attempt.

Several key officers of the General Staff made known their strong objections to the operation and begged Lon Nol not to launch it while the military was still weakened as a result of Chenla I. They pointed out that it would take time to see that new recruits were properly trained, but Lon Nol believed all they needed to deflect enemy bullets was to wear amulets and sacred cloths prepared by Mam Prum Mony. Just as in the Chenla I operation, troops stretched out in a long, thin line were promptly decimated by the combined forces of the Viet Cong, North Vietnamese, and Khmer Rouge.

Government casualties were high, with some of the best infantry units decimated. Large numbers of government troops fled across rice fields, abandoning equipment, including tanks, 105mm howitzers, and countless light weapons. A few years later, Khmer Rouge forces used these weapons to attack the city of Phnom Penh. These losses broke the spirit of the Cambodian army, which never seemed to recover from this crushing defeat.

Lon Nol, on the other hand, did indeed seem to be living in the "fairyland" realm described earlier by General Sutsakhan. In his Order of the Day issued to government troops on 5 October 1971, Lon Nol told his men that since the launching of Chenla II on 20 August,

> you have overcome the enemy and destroyed his finest regiments. The enemy has been put to flight, leaving on the field irreparable damage. The morale of the enemy is surely very low. Your exploits have exceeded our hopes, and you have held high the flag of the Republic. Humbly I bow before your dead. Their sacrifices are not in vain.

****

From my perspective today, I can easily see what I could not fully comprehend at the time; that is, the gradual unraveling of the Cambodian government and its inability to face the truth of what was happening throughout the country. Many citizens could perceive this disintegration and doubted the government's ability to reform from within. Fearful of what was to come, those who had money and education fled the country. At the same time, thousands of poor refugees began pouring into Phnom Penh, telling of the devastation caused by American bombs and by the reign of terror that characterized life in regions controlled by the Khmer Rouge. Sadly, none of this was heeded by those in power. Lon Nol never listened to his own people or to his military commanders.

I believe that it was this sense of futility, and the knowledge that our society was in the process of decomposition, that led otherwise honorable people to take drastic means to survive. Provincial governors and military commanders began destroying forests and selling wood to the Thais, and even selling arms and munitions to the Khmer Rouge. Commanders in the field allowed the Khmer Rouge to operate within their sphere of operations in exchange for promises not to attack their outposts. In addition, Lon Nol's government began to purchase rubber from plantations controlled by the Khmer Rouge in order to sell it abroad.

In 1972, Lon Nol presented himself as a candidate for president in elections widely considered to be fraudulent. Little Brother boasted publicly that he had increased Lon Nol's victory by at least twenty percentage points over his two main opponents combined.

In March 1973, Little Brother's ruffians used grenades to break up a strike by teachers, after which all schools and universities were closed. During the next year, there were times when the General's life was in danger from those angered by his policies. At one time, bombs hit the residence, and in a second incident, bombs landed where he was attending a meeting in Phnom Penh. These bombs came not from enemy positions around the city but from planes flown by Khmer Air Force officers sickened by the regime's corruption and incompetency. Although neither the General nor others in his entourage saw these events as symptomatic of the depth of animosity people felt toward those in power, every fiber of our society was unraveling long before the Khmer Rouge took over.

When I was young, I truly believed that the Buddha sent powerful energies to protect all rulers of the Khmer people, and that their subjects could never touch or look upon such powerful rulers. Most people who lived outside of Phnom Penh and who earned their livelihood from the land and rivers believed they owed their livelihood and loyalty to these rulers. Without these men chosen by the Buddha, the rains would not come, the rivers would not change their course, and the crops would not grow. Eventually, however, I came to realize that no king, prince, president, or general receives any more powerful energies and blessings than the Buddha grants to all other sentient beings. All creation is equal in that respect.

I regret that General Lon Nol was never able to face the reality of the situation. While thousands of refugees coming into the capital testified to the devastation caused by U.S. bombing, as well as Khmer Rouge atrocities, Lon Nol kept requesting what he termed "aerial assistance" (i.e., bombing raids) from the United States.

In one letter, he told President Nixon that the enemy was following a scorched earth policy, resulting in "a horrible spectacle of ruin, of suffering, and of mourning in our civilian population and among our Buddhist monks." In another letter, Lon Nol described "the systematic burning of houses; massacres of men, women, children...and monks"; and the use of "toxic gas against our soldiers and civilian population," a claim that I do not believe was ever substantiated. I do not know if Lon Nol ever considered that the bombing missions he valued so highly might have caused the havoc and carnage he so vividly described to President Nixon.

When, in mid-1973, Little Brother left for an extended visit to the United States, rumors circulated in the city that the Americans would try to prevent him from returning to Cambodia. Many believed the Americans were trying to remove Lon Nol as well, but it was hard to separate fact from rumor in those days. Now, in looking through the correspondence between Lon Nol and Richard Nixon, I can see that the U.S.

president was indeed urging the General to visit America, both for health treatments and for direct meetings to discuss strategy. I can imagine how difficult it must have been for the General to turn down the president's invitation, which he may well have seen as a ploy by the Americans to remove him or diminish his authority. In a rambling and emotional letter dated 12 July 1973, Lon Nol thanked President Nixon for his "multiple continuing, untiring, and fruitful efforts to assist us in restoring peace...." He added:

> You, Mr. President, [have] earned the admiration and respect of the entire world. [Your] distinguished qualities arouse the admiration of the peoples of the world and make you the most outstanding figure of contemporary history. I thank you for the invitation to visit the U.S., but in view of the gravity of the situation, I believe it would not be wise to leave the country at this time.

In another letter sent to Nixon later that same month, Lon Nol expressed a desire to make a strong case for international support for his government at the September 1973 United Nations General Assembly. President Nixon replied:

> I believe your case will be immeasurably strengthened if you can report a record of bold and dynamic leadership and substantial progress in resolving the internal military and administrative problems that still confront the [Khmer] Republic.

Lon Nol responded with a promise to "draw up and execute a plan of action to rectify our errors and failures."

In late August 1973, President Nixon admitted to Lon Nol that the U.S. Congress precluded him from providing any further air support to the Khmer Republic. He wrote, "The Khmer Republic's survival rests on [its] own efforts to galvanize the population and energetically implement measures to strengthen its military and political position."

Throughout the summer of 1974, Nol repeatedly told Nixon of the gains by enemy forces. He refrained, as he had done before, from identifying the enemy as the Khmer Rouge.

> Our enemies are bombarding wantonly all of Phnom Penh with rockets and cannons....The North Vietnamese are still in our country and are running the offensive against us....If the Khmer people become exhausted [by attacks against them], the North Vietnamese will dominate the country.

Just days before the American president resigned in disgrace, Richard Nixon sent his last letter to Lon Nol, never mentioning the gravity of his own situation:

> I am confident that under your vigorous leadership, the Republic will succeed. I congratulate you and your people for the many recent military successes under your inspirational leadership. With warmest personal regards.
> Sincerely,
> Richard Nixon.

****

Once he learned of President Nixon's forced resignation, the General's faith was shaken, and the irrevocable ascent of the Khmer Rouge increased in intensity, beginning with constant, random shelling of Phnom Penh.

One morning, as I was walking toward the Central Market to procure medicines for the General, there was a loud whooshing sound, followed by a deafening crash. I fell to the ground to avoid being hit by flying shrapnel. Once I felt it safe to stand up and move about, I could see nothing but black smoke billowing up from the area of the market. People were running away in fright, many of them wounded and in shock. As I moved closer to the scene, I saw sights of such horror that I began to howl like one possessed by an evil spirit, but no one could hear me because the sound emanating from my throat was drowned out by the screams and moans of others around me.

There were pieces of flesh and bone as well as parts of human bodies all around—in the nearby trees, among broken stalls and shattered fruit, on top of cars and *cyclos*, and all over the bloodied pavement. On the ground near the stall where Cham women sold silk fabrics, I saw a beautiful piece of sapphire blue silk on which rested the delicate hand of a young girl wearing a ring of the same blue color. There was no blood on the silk fabric—only the lovely hand resting peacefully amid the horror.

Like a drunken man, I staggered around and walked aimlessly through the city until I came to the National Museum. I often came to this place to meditate in the stillness of the peaceful courtyard of the Leper King. On that day, someone had placed over one shoulder of the statue a long orange cloth, of the same color and material of robes worn by monks. I knelt down in front of this comforting statue and prayed to the Buddha the chant that I continue to say seven times every hour that I am awake: *Namo—Sambuddhassa! Buddham Damman! Sangham!* (Praise Be to Him, the Blessed One, the Fully Enlightened One! Teachings of Buddha, be our refuge! Monks, be our protectors!)

I cried and prayed while looking into the compassionate face of the Leper King, in words very similar to those later used by the Cambodian poet U Sam Oeur, who lived through the monstrous reign of Pol Pot:

> Look down on us, O gods of the land!
> My people, men and women, suffer beyond words.
> Open your magic eyes, O Father!
> Look at Cambodia! Liberate my people!
> They are in Hell: children, elders, men, women.
> O God, free us from agony and fear!

****

Probably at the urging of the Americans, Lon Nol initiated some attempts to negotiate with the Khmer Rouge, but Pol Pot never responded because he controlled most of the country and would soon take over the capital as well.

Weeks before Lon Nol's departure, a rocket landed in a huge ammunition dump near the airport, sending twenty tons of explosives into the air and leading many residents of Phnom Penh to believe the whole city was being destroyed. Rockets and howitzer shells slammed into the city all through the day and night. At one point, the army began cutting down trees along one of the main boulevards to serve as an emergency landing strip in case the airport closed down completely.

One morning, Lon Nol informed his staff that he would be receiving an important delegation of members of his government. Rumors had already been circulating within the residence that these men planned to ask the General to step aside. The General did not tell us what transpired during the visit, but we later learned that his colleagues finally convinced him that his departure might be the only way they could achieve true negotiations with the Khmer Rouge.

In anticipation of what he had feared and expected for several months, the General had earlier asked his friend, President Suharto of Indonesia, to extend him an invitation to spend a two-week vacation on the island of Bali. Using this as a pretext for leaving Phnom Penh, the General informed us that any of us who wished to join him on this vacation trip were welcome to do so.

None of the monks on the General's staff agreed to accompany him. They knew the risks they were taking, but love for their country outweighed any fear they had of the Khmer Rouge. These men never could have foreseen how brutally Buddhist monks would be treated under the Pol Pot regime. I was prepared to stay as well, but the General entreated me to go with him by invoking the memory of my dead mother, who was close to his beloved first wife. I believe, in hindsight, that I represented his only link with that happier period of his life. Keeping to the vow I had made to my mother, I agreed to leave with the General.

Several rockets exploded close to our airplane as a tearful Lon Nol finally left the country. After a two-week stay in Bali, we went to Hawaii, where the General remained for several years before moving to California. Before he made that final move, I informed the General of my desire to go to Thailand to work with refugees fleeing the Khmer Rouge, and eventually to take my final vows as a Buddhist monk. After giving me the leather case containing his correspondence with President Nixon, he gave me enough money to pay for my travel to Thailand and to help those working with the refugees.

Once airborne en route to Bangkok, I felt a great burden lifted from me. I was also greatly relieved to be away from the General's mean-spirited wife, who distrusted me and everyone else in her husband's entourage. She and her son, as well as seven offspring of the General's lesser wives, lived in the same building in Hawaii, where she ruled over every aspect of the household. She and her son were especially harsh toward the other children, whom she had tried to prevent from joining them as they left Phnom Penh. She often berated her husband for allowing those children, whom she treated as slaves, to live under her roof.

Thanks to the money the General had given me, I found people in Bangkok who could lead me to a refugee camp administered by Buddhist monks who escaped from Cambodia. Each day and night we chanted our prayers to the Buddha, seeking his compassionate care for the wounded, maimed, starving, and frightened people in our care. Among these poor victims and with the support of the monks, I felt more at peace than at any other time in my life. When I was young, I was not sure whether I wanted to remain in the monastery; but now, after all the places that life had taken me, I knew I had found my place in the world.

I experienced true happiness in my work with the refugees, my dear countrymen who had suffered so much. Like the Buddha under the *bodhi* tree, I learned that enlightenment can occur in ordinary places. I was now living out the sacred vows I would take as soon as I returned to our ravaged land to complete my training as a monk.

Once back in Cambodia, I was relieved that Pol Pot was gone, but officials of that murderous regime still retain power over us. We are not yet a free people able to choose our own leaders. Families will forever remain torn apart by the widespread massacres inflicted by the Khmer Rouge. I am especially saddened to see that many have lost their interest in religion and no longer value those aspects of our Khmer culture that make us unique.

When I took my final vows, I repeated the words, "I vow to attain enlightenment (*bodhi*) for the sake of all sentient beings (*sattva*)." I pray that fear and hatred will one day be transformed into hope and compassion. I believe that the earth and all who inhabit it are bound together in one single story and destiny. By making the earth beautiful and productive, restoring ruined temples, healing our brothers and sisters, and rebuilding our shattered society, we can reclaim our traditional values. The hearts of our people cannot be changed by facts or things, but only by hope, visions, dreams, and a return to the teachings of the Buddha. Humans alone cannot achieve any of this without the Buddha.

****

Chapter 2

Sophana's Story
by Thoun Sophana

"Where are you going?" my mother asked. I did not respond because I knew she was not listening. My father was in his other residence, where he lived with one of his mistresses. As a senior official of the National Bank, he took advantage of the system of cronyism and patronage that characterized our antiquated feudal government, which served to enrich those such as my father, while ignoring the needs of the people of Cambodia. My parents were unaware that I had joined a new political organization whose aim was to create a communist utopia where all would share equally in the wealth of the nation. Although our ruler, Prince Norodom Sihanouk, referred to members of this organization by the pejorative French term *Khmers Rouges* (Red Khmers), those words came to represent a rallying cry I was proud to invoke.

I ran down the staircase, two steps at a time, sliding my hand over the smooth banister as the first rays of sun shone on the polished tile floor and cream-colored walls of our villa. With each step, I felt I was leaving the night and my childhood behind. As I looked around me, the feeling of alienation from my parents and surroundings intensified. This Sunday morning in June 1960 was one of those moments when I realized how

45

fortunate I was. I was a free, independent person; I had recently graduated from the prestigious Lycée Sisowath; the young man I loved would soon return from Paris; and I was a member of the Communist Women's Organization led by my teacher, an impressive revolutionary role model named Khieu Ponnary.

Because it was Sunday, I decided to walk down toward the riverbank where people gathered during the early morning hours. Ever since the French installed their so-called protectorate in Cambodia in 1863 (ostensibly to prevent the Thais and Vietnamese from further incursions into our country, but actually to open a lucrative trade route for themselves to China via the Mekong River), they imposed many of their own institutions and traditions onto our Khmer culture and way of life. The best of these French traditions was the concept of Sunday as a day of rest. For residents of Phnom Penh, the day always took on an especially festive aura.

Before continuing toward the riverbank, I made my way to the top of Wat Phnom to make an offering to Yeay Penh (Lady Penh), the woman responsible for the creation of this sacred site and for the name of our city. Legend tells us that she was a wealthy woman who, in 1379, pulled a floating Koki tree out of the river and discovered four Buddha statues inside the tree. She had a *phnom* (hill) built in the city, atop of which a *wat* (pagoda) was designed to house the four Buddha statues. Centuries later, rulers changed the city's name to Penh's Hill, or Phnom Penh. I was proud to live in a city named for a woman and often prayed at the shrine of Lady Penh.

I descended the hill as the full morning sun rose over the spacious residences within the Royal Palace grounds. It seemed a special privilege to witness the awakening of these magical palaces and pagodas with their black- and gold-trimmed orange tile roofs. The corner of each pitched roof ended in antler-shaped lintels whose coiled arcs reminded me of the tails of sleeping dragons.

Meandering along and thinking about the future, I felt in the pocket of my sarong the most recent letter from my fiancé, Thoun Hak, who was completing his law degree in Paris. I knew that Hak was involved in leftist political activities but could not discuss it. We had agreed to avoid political matters in our correspondence because we knew the secret police monitored the mail of students abroad. When I reached into my pocket, the letter from Hak crinkled slightly at my touch, reminding me how much I looked forward to his return.

Pondering the many exciting possibilities for the future, I looked out toward the wide boulevards lined with *flamboyant* trees, whose arches of orange flowers matched the orange tiles of the royal residences. Along my route, I breathed in the sweet scent of jasmine, frangipani, and other tropical flowers surrounding the stately ochre and cream colonial villas lining the boulevard. At the same time, I felt deep revulsion for the extravagant lives of those such as my parents who inhabited these palatial homes. Opposite me, I saw a line of barefoot Buddhist monks in orange robes making their early morning rounds and holding out their copper bowls, silently begging for rice or money to aid the poor.

My spirits soared when I heard a familiar voice calling my name, "Sophana! Prak Sophana! Over here!" It was Hak's younger sister Vanny, who had also joined the Communist Women's Organization when we completed our secondary school studies. Vanny studied at the Lycée Norodom while I attended the more prestigious Lycée Sisowath.

"I was hoping to see you here! I have been so busy planning my wedding that I had forgotten to contact my friends. Speaking of weddings, have you heard from Hak? I can't wait until you two are married and we can be sisters!"

After I shared the contents of Hak's letter with her, Vanny said, "I have some disturbing news about someone we both admire."

She took from her shoulder bag a newspaper on whose front page was a photo of the young journalist Khieu Samphan. (Although their families were close, there was no family relationship between Khieu Samphan and Khieu Ponnary, head of the Communist Women's Organization.) Upon his return from doctoral studies in Paris, Samphan had started a French-language journal, *L'Observateur*, in which he spoke empathetically of the hardships of peasants and workers. I cried when I read his latest article exposing the misery of child laborers in Phnom Penh, whom Samphan described as having been "deprived of the joys of youth" and "wearing the faces of old people."

As we looked at the photo of Samphan, Vanny exclaimed in a low voice, "See what the police have done to Samphan! He was pulled from his bicycle as he left his office last night and was beaten, stripped, and put into prison for his anti-government editorials."

"Just look at his battered body and bloodied face! This will only attract more young people and intellectuals to the communist movement. The longer they keep Samphan, the louder the protests will become! While I feel a bit afraid of what the future holds for us, I believe that whatever sacrifices we may have to make will ultimately lead to a better life for future generations of Cambodians. Long live the Khmer Rouge revolution! Long live Khieu Samphan!"

"Keep your voice down, Sophana! Lon Nol's secret police are everywhere, seeking out sympathizers of Khieu Samphan and the Khmer Rouge."

"That was stupid of me! I promise to be more careful in the future. Because Samphan's family is wealthy and his father a well-known judge with ties to the royal palace, I doubt the police will hold Samphan for too long. They also know that there would be riots in the streets if Samphan were killed."

Vanny placed the newspaper back into her bag. We had now arrived at the banks of the Tonle Sap River, which joins the Mekong River south of the city. The riverbank provided a delightful spectacle: graceful, gilded black and red dragon boats moored in front of the royal boathouse; the parade of families, couples, and groups of young people; and vendors offering balloons, kites, flowers, and a variety of specialty foods. There was so much to choose from, including grilled fish stuffed with dried shrimp and wrapped in lettuce leaves dipped in pepper sauce; fried noodles with pickled mango strips; and baguette sandwiches stuffed with sliced meat, cucumbers, green onion, and cilantro. For dessert, there were fried bananas dipped in sugar and crêpes filled with mango and cinnamon, as well as all kinds of fruits and ice cream.

After we finished our crêpes, formed into cones and placed into lacy paper napkins, we sipped tea at another stall next to a café frequented by French residents of Phnom Penh. The French owner had turned on the radio, which was playing an anti-war song by a chanteuse named Barbara. This song echoed the sentiments of those tired of the French involvement in a never-ending war in Vietnam and the growing French military involvement in Algeria. The chanteuse was accompanied by a solitary drumbeat that grew louder and louder, until it drowned out her words at the end of the song. The French people sitting in the café accompanied the drumbeat by pounding their fists on the tables. I may not remember all the words exactly, but this closely resembles what Vanny and I heard that Sunday morning.

Down through the ages, the relentless refrain;
Angry gods and bloodthirsty kings
Trying to build a heaven on earth
By slaughtering enemies and breaking their bones.
But the wars never cease and the blood still flows.
Angry gods and bloodthirsty kings
Never bring peace, and the wars never cease.

After listening to the French song with its disconcerting references to angry gods and wars, we talked about the trip we had attended in April.

****

Our trip was organized by the Communist Women's Organization and took us to the temples of Angkor Thom and Angkor Wat, over three hundred miles northwest of Phnom Penh.

While we gazed up at the huge Buddhist-inspired Angkor Thom monuments, our guide proudly pointed to several enormous pineapple-shaped stone towers crowned by heads with four large, sublime faces, each looking out toward a different direction. The guide explained, "These are faces of truth, whose field of vision encompasses everything good or evil that has affected the Khmer people over the centuries. Nothing escapes the eyes of these faces with their smiles of infinite wisdom and compassion."

When we moved on to the Hindu-inspired temples of Angkor Wat, we studied the bas-relief sculptures, depicting scenes from the Indian epic of violence, the *Ramayana* (*Ream-ker* in Khmer). These scenes of men stabbing, lancing, and clubbing each other disturbed me for days. Carvings on other walls depicted a fierce naval battle in which the Khmers defeated the Muslim Chams while crocodiles devoured drowning men. For many nights after the visit, I had disturbing dreams of the ancient god-kings of Cambodia returning, still thirsting for more blood and death.

During the trip to Angkor, our guide pointed out that the significance of Angkor Wat was not only the magnificent temples, but also the irrigation system associated with these temples. Each king brought in slaves from remote northern tribes both to erect a temple to hold his ashes and to dig out canals and moats linking the new temple with the rest of the royal city. As the guide noted, Cambodia suffered for centuries from too much water when the Mekong flooded (mid-June to November), and not enough water for the rest of the year, thus making it impossible to produce more than one rice crop per year.

French scientists of the late nineteenth and early twentieth century concluded that the builders of Angkor used the moats and canals, as well as huge tanks held up by earthen dikes, to store water for irrigating the land during the dry season, thereby increasing the yield to two or three rice harvests per year. Recent research indicates that the farmers of ancient Angkor also grew flood recession rice around the lake, as well as wet season rice further from the shore, in order to achieve two rice harvests per year. When the Khmer Rouge forced city people into the countryside in 1975 to build canals and irrigation systems, they thought this would yield a glorious "three tons per hectare," but they did not listen to farmers who knew about irrigation and rice production. Instead, they created a ridiculous grid system that never worked, thus destroying their dream of a communist utopia that would become the world's largest rice exporter.

On the last night of the visit to Angkor, Vanny and I were thrilled when the young journalist Khieu Samphan appeared and began to address our group. Wearing a red and white *krama* around his neck and dressed all in black, he looked striking. His inspiring words exhorted us to take part in a communist revolution to revitalize our country by creating a new society built on the ideas of equality and mutual assistance between the city people and rural people. What soaring ideals he evoked, and how we wanted to follow in the path he described!

****

After walking along the river in the hot sun on that lovely Sunday morning, we hailed a three-wheeled pedicab, or *cyclo*, driven by a scrawny, leathery-skinned man wearing a *krama*, the checked scarf worn by peasants and by members of the Khmer Rouge as a symbol of their support for the peasants. The driver brought us to the cool, stone-paved square in front of the Post and Telegraph building, at the opposite end of which sits the Hotel de la Poste with its awning-trimmed outdoor café known as La Taverne.

From our vantage point at one corner of the café, we noticed Khieu Ponnary, Ieng Thirith, and their respective husbands, Saloth Sar and Ieng Sary, approaching. They kept their heads down and seemed to be engrossed in a deep conversation, probably regarding the arrest of Khieu Samphan. As Thirith swept by on her way to a table at the other end of the café, I could hear the jingling of bracelets and detect the scent of a lovely rose-based soap or perfume she had probably bought when she and her husband were students in Paris. I also noticed her long, delicate, manicured fingers covered in rings, likely from the ruby and sapphire mines in Pailin Province where her family owned property.

Vanny noted the beads of perspiration along Ieng Sary's upper lip and large domed forehead. "Do you see how his shirt clings under his arms and along his back in large patches of sweat? He probably does not have a very pleasant odor! I will never understand how such a fastidious woman as Ieng Thirith could have chosen him as her husband. I have heard that soon after her arrival in Paris she became pregnant, but Sary wanted her to have an abortion. They eventually married, presumably after much pressure and financial assistance from her influential family."

"Hak told me that Sary's real name is Kim Trang but that he changed it to a more Khmer-sounding name."

"Yes, but his light complexion indicates some Chinese ancestry, as does Sar's. Sar's facial features, however, are much more rounded and open like those of a true Khmer, reminiscent of those faces on the monuments at Angkor Thom. While Sary seems devious, his brother-in-law appears much more approachable."

"I agree. The sisters made surprising choices for husbands!" Unlike Ieng Sary, Sar seemed cool in his short-sleeved clean white shirt, with no trace of perspiration on his body or clothes.

Ponnary, who always carried herself modestly, sat next to her sister at the table, and directly opposite Saloth Sar. Her traditional Khmer clothes, sarong and sleeveless blouse, were drab but well cared for. At times she hid her face behind her hands while her husband spoke, smiling quietly or nodding her head, as if she already knew by heart what he was saying.

Ponnary was the first Cambodian girl to graduate from the Lycée Sisowath, a school heretofore reserved for the French, as well as young Cambodian men deemed by the French as worthy of such an elite education. Ponnary's younger sister Thirith, a graduate of the same school, was also intelligent, tough, and determined.

Taking advantage of Khmer government-sponsored scholarships for university studies in France, both sisters chose to go to the Sorbonne in Paris. There they expressed their defiance against French policies toward Cambodia by refusing to study French literature. Ponnary majored in Khmer history and literature, which she taught upon her return to Cambodia. Thirith, who majored in English literature with a focus on the works of Shakespeare, also became a teacher and founded an English-language school in Phnom Penh.

Thirith preferred Western dress and hairstyles and referred to herself not as Khieu Thirith but as Ieng Thirith, following the Western practice of a wife assuming the husband's family name. I had a visceral dislike for Thirith's husband, Ieng Sary, who was a Khmer Krom—Khmer people from the Mekong Delta, which had been annexed by the Vietnamese. The Khmer Krom never seemed to be at home anywhere; the Vietnamese hated them and the Cambodians mistrusted them. My mother often referred to them as "people with Khmer bodies and Vietnamese minds."

In contrast to her sister and to most Cambodian women, Khieu Ponnary wore no jewels, nor did she dress in flattering, feminine attire. Some of her students referred to her privately as "the old virgin." She kept her hair cut in the short, blunt Chinese style, and her face bore the scars of smallpox she had as a child. When she spoke, however, she was always interesting and sincere. Both Khieu Ponnary and Ieng Thirith met their future husbands in Paris.

After a beautiful young woman had rejected his offer of marriage, Saloth Sar decided to take advantage of his palace connections to obtain a scholarship to a technical school in Paris. Even with that opportunity, he failed in his studies of radio-electronics, preferring instead to read French poetry and enjoy his newfound freedom. One night, at a meeting in Ieng Sary's hotel room, Sar met Khieu Ponnary, the sister of Ieng Sary's pregnant wife. After speaking with this intelligent woman, he decided that she was the woman he must marry.

At that time, Ponnary was thirty-one, and Saloth Sar only twenty-three. It is extremely rare for a Cambodian man to marry an older woman, and equally rare for a woman from a good family to marry a man with no obvious prospects. Sar and Ponnary eventually married in Phnom Penh on Bastille Day, the anniversary of the French Revolution.

****

My parents' fortune flourished under the regime of Norodom Sihanouk. My father's ascent within the National Bank could never have occurred without his taking advantage of the various forms of bribery and corruption that characterized all levels of Cambodian political and business circles. With my father's rise to prominence, my mother relished the role of the traditional Khmer wife as chief of the family and its finances, within a culture where the husband brings home money and hands it to his wife.

I recall my mother trying to instruct me in the benefits of this way of life. Even as a small child, however, I questioned the wisdom of such a system. She often told me the story of Queen Neang Neak who reigned during the earliest days of our nation, known then as Funan.

When the Indian Prince Kaodinha, or Preah Thong in Khmer, conquered Funan, he married Neang Neak. He followed the queen throughout the ceremony, holding onto her scarf to avoid being distracted by his surroundings. At all royal wedding ceremonies since that time, the groom holds onto the bride's scarf throughout the ceremony.

"Doesn't it seem unnecessary to keep doing it today unless the groom happens to be blind or unable to walk on his own?"

"You don't understand, Sophana. We maintain this tradition because it recognizes the importance of Khmer women in society. The husband is guided in all things by his wife and always heeds her advice and counsel."

"If women are so important, why aren't there any women in important positions in Cambodia?"

"That is because a woman's power must be restricted to the confines of the home. The wives of important men can bend their husbands to their will. Remember the maxims I have repeated to you many times: 'If you are a colonel, your wife must be a general,' and 'A husband's disapproval plus the wife's approval equals approval.' That is the way Cambodian women maintain our power and importance."

As I observed my mother and others of her generation, I saw that a woman becomes increasingly formidable as her husband assumes higher rank. She is then in a position to grant favors and assistance to her friends and to the wives of her husband's subordinates. Such assistance, however, does not come without strings attached, as the cycle of bribery and intrigue continues. The venue for my mother's display of her prominence was the weekly meeting at our home. The women played cards while engaging in veiled conversations of flattery and supplication, to be met either by my mother's magnanimous granting of favors or her silent disregard of the supplicant and her request.

The more familiar I became with this closed, mean-spirited society of women, the more I wanted to escape from it. The type of woman I admired was Khieu Ponnary who rejected outward signs of luxury and worked as an equal with her husband in trying to improve Cambodian society. Because of my admiration for Ponnary, I began to emulate her in dress and demeanor, something that clearly exasperated my mother.

During a special meeting of the Communist Women's Organization in September 1960, Ponnary informed us that the Cambodian communists had recently convened their first party congress. She explained that Sihanouk's efforts to wipe out all pockets of resistance had only led to a desire for revenge on the part of the communists and, in her words, a "burning hatred" that, once kindled, would not be easily extinguished. Leaders of the new Khmer Rouge movement vowed to create a true Marxist-Leninist party similar to that espoused by their allies, the communist leaders in Vietnam. The three-day party congress, attended by twenty-two representatives from the various regions, took place in a closed section of the Phnom Penh railroad station to avoid detection by government forces.

Ponnary identified for us the key precepts decided upon at the party congress: independence, national sovereignty, and self-reliance. Later I learned of another important precept hidden from us at that time; namely, revolutionary violence.

****

Despite the fact that my fiancé Hak was away in Paris to complete his law degree, my life seemed to overflow with happiness and potential. The Communist Women's Organization was pleased with my work distributing leaflets, and I had found a rewarding job at the National Museum. All these promising developments made it easier to deal with Hak's absence and my parents' lack of interest in my life.

I loved my work in the cataloging department of the National Museum, only steps away from the Lycée Sisowath. When she learned of my position at the museum, Khieu Ponnary asked me to assume a needed task for the Khmer Rouge organization. She believed that the museum could serve as a useful venue for receiving messages exchanged between party leaders in Phnom Penh and those in the countryside. After handing me these messages, couriers would give me instructions for delivery to clandestine party intermediaries who would meet me at designated areas of the museum. I eagerly took on this task, which reflected the trust that Khieu Ponnary placed in me.

Many evening meetings of senior party officials took place either at the Lycée Sisowath or in the cloistered courtyards of the museum. Participants waited until the thousands of bats living under the museum's roofs flocked out and swarmed around the sky searching for insects. That was the signal for members to gather and receive directions to proceed to either the Lycée or the Museum.

The museum's elderly curator, Nhem Samchay, was a long-time family friend of Khieu Ponnary and her sister Ieng Thirith, to whom he granted private access for these evening meetings. I learned much about our rich Khmer culture and history from this venerable man. For that reason, I instinctively began to address him not merely as *Lok* Samchay (Mr. Samchay), but as *Lok kru* Samchay, a respectful form of address reserved for teachers.

Each time I entered the lovely terra-cotta museum with its pitched wooden roofs and antler-like finials that echoed those of the Royal Palace buildings, I marveled at its beauty. In very bright light the building takes on a pink tone, while at other times it assumes a purple hue. Designed by French architect

Georges Groslier and inaugurated by King Monivong in 1920, it follows traditional Khmer architectural designs, far removed from the ugly modern edifices that began to appear during the 1960s under Sihanouk's reign. I hated the huge chocolate-hued Independence Monument, as well as the concrete Bassac Theater and National Sports Center, built in the so-called neo-Khmer style to celebrate what Sihanouk referred to as the Golden Age, marking the end of French rule.

The museum's elegant exterior is surpassed only by the palm-shaded interior, whose central courtyard and peaceful lotus ponds surround the famous statue of the Leper King. Although other sections of the museum contain thousands of priceless individual pieces and collections of Khmer art dating back to the sixth century, the courtyard of the Leper King always drew me to it. Unlike other Khmer statuary, this figure is naked. Another unique feature is that the subject is in a seated position, with the right knee raised while the upturned right arm, whose hand is missing, rests on that knee. On his face is a serene, enigmatic smile.

Nhem Samchay told me that this statue once stood on a terrace at Angkor Thom, built under the reign of King Jayavarman VII (1183–1201). One day, I showed the elderly curator the notes taken during my student trip to Angkor, specifically the notes from the inscription on the stele of Jayavarman VII, which read:

He suffered more
From his subjects' diseases
Than from his own.
For it is the people's pain
That makes the pain of kings,
And not their own.

"*Lok kru*, because these words were carved into the stele of the great King of Angkor, does this mean that the Leper King was Jayavarman VII?"

"I doubt that, Sophana, although mystery and uncertainty have long surrounded the origin of this statue. It is not certain that Jayavarman VII was indeed a leper, although many deduced this to be the case because of all the hospitals he had built during his reign. Some experts believe that the statue depicted Kubera, god of wealth, or King Yasovarman I, who may have been a leper. Other experts, having analyzed 14th and 15th century inscriptions on the statue, believe the figure to be Yama, god of death or of judgment. Another theory is that the lichen and moss growing on the statue resemble the skin of a person with leprosy. As for me, I prefer to refer to the seated figure as Dharmaraja, the name etched at the bottom of the statue."

"In any case, *Lok kru*, I prefer to think of this exquisite figure simply as the Leper King who suffered from his subject's diseases and pain, a beautiful image that is certainly not exemplified by our own ruling monarch."

While I knew that Nhem Samchay was critical of Prince Sihanouk, I did not want to criticize him too openly, for fear of detection by one of Lon Nol's ubiquitous spies. Unlike the Leper King, Sihanouk was a vain man who seemed to have no interest in the difficulties and pain of his people. While peasants starved in the countryside and young children labored like slaves even in Phnom Penh, Norodom Sihanouk amused himself by directing, producing, and acting in films, featuring him and members of the government and court.

****

I never told Nhem Samchay that I belonged to the Communist Women's Organization, but I do not believe he would have minded, given his disapproval of Prince Sihanouk. At one of the organization's meetings, Khieu Ponnary announced that our colleague, Eng Maly, would be leaving soon for Beijing. Maly, from an ethnic Chinese family, attended a secondary school where instructors taught in both Khmer and Chinese. Although we attended different schools, I considered her a friend and enjoyed talking with her whenever I visited the stall in the Central Market (*Phsar Thmei*) where she assisted her father, who treated ill people with herbal infusions and other forms of traditional Chinese medicine. Ponnary asked

Maly to explain why she would be going to Beijing and what she hoped to learn there.

"After working with my father, I decided I want to learn more about Chinese medicine, specifically to specialize in treating diseases of the mind. I also wish to see for myself the results of Chairman Mao Tse Tung's efforts to reshape Chinese society and create a truly Chinese form of communism. My parents and I are great admirers of Chairman Mao."

"This is a wonderful opportunity, Maly. When you return, we look forward to learning more from you concerning Chairman Mao's policies, which our Cambodian form of communism would like to emulate. My husband and I have been impressed with what we have learned concerning Chairman Mao's efforts to mobilize labor, improve agricultural and industrial productivity, and organize people into collectives where all share equally in the wealth of the nation."

Although many years have passed since that day when Eng Maly explained the reasons for her visit to China, I remember clearly Ponnary turning to our group as a whole and expounding on other world revolutionary movements and the importance of the revolution we were all hoping to bring about in Cambodia. Although these words are not exactly what Ponnary said that day, they represent the essence of her address:

My dear young women, since founding this organization I have sought to impress upon you the important role you will play in our own Cambodian revolution that we are in the process of creating. To prepare you for this task, you have read and memorized the precepts of Marx, Lenin, Stalin, and Mao Tse Tung. We have paid special attention to Stalin's emphasis on the need for continual self-criticism, as well as vigilance and internal purges to keep the party pure. Like Stalin before him, Chairman Mao believes in the need to destroy all aspects of bourgeois capitalism and remnants of an outdated feudal society.

Other earlier revolutions can also inspire us today. You might be surprised to hear that one of these, the French Revolution of 1789, offers a model worth studying. At that time, France contained three societal divisions: religion, the monarchy, and the common people. Today in Cambodia, we have three similar divisions: Buddhism, the royalty and ruling elite, and everyone else. Those of us who studied in France came to admire Maximilien Robespierre whom we saw as a pure revolutionary, not merely the architect of what many refer to as the Reign of Terror. To be a true revolutionary in the model of Robespierre is to acknowledge that there is no middle way or compromise. Once a revolution begins, we must push forward to its conclusion, the result being better than what went before.

In an especially urgent and strong tone of voice, Ponnary concluded,

Unfortunately, Robespierre's revolution never fully succeeded. His enemies within the movement turned against him and sent him to the guillotine. Worse yet, his movement built on revolutionary ideals was followed by a restoration of the monarchy. We cannot afford to let this happen in Cambodia!

****

I looked forward to the day when Cambodia would have its own revolution. Like other young educated Cambodians, I saw no hope for us in the continuation of our corrupt feudal system of government. Eager to find any alternative, we enthusiastically followed role models such as Khieu Ponnary and Khieu Samphan, whose words and example inspired us.

I was overjoyed when my fiancé Hak returned from Paris in March 1962, a year later than we had anticipated because his well-received dissertation had required further extensive research. Upon his return, Hak accepted an assignment to serve as an assistant to Khieu Samphan while also teaching law at the University of Phnom Penh. Hak's arrival coincided with the annual Water Festival, a three-day event when uninhibited revelers fill the streets day and night, often drinking to excess, and when public flirtation on the part of young people is condoned and even encouraged. Throughout the festivities, Phnom Penh takes on an increasingly frenzied ambience as the floodwaters of the great Tonle Sap Lake, engorged by the annual monsoon rains, cause it to overflow and reverse course downward toward the mouth of the Mekong and out to sea. While watching the dragon boat races, Hak and I enjoyed kissing in public, cheered on by Vanny and her new husband.

Since his return, Hak and I worked together for our clandestine political organizations. It was wonderful to have my feelings of love reciprocated by this tall young man who was the brother of my best friend, and to know that he was associated with Khieu Samphan, the person who epitomized my ideal of a pure revolutionary. I asked Hak to tell me what he had learned in Paris about Samphan.

"Members of the Cambodian Marxist Circle admire Samphan for his incorruptibility but doubt he will ever assume a top position within the party. This is mainly because of his effeminate manner and his regularly playing girls' roles in the student dance company, which members of the Marxist Circle see as a sign of weakness. While they know Samphan's popularity will attract new members, they believe it unlikely that other party leaders will ever accord him a role of real authority."

"I am disappointed by hearing this, Hak. Members of communist youth groups in Phnom Penh admire his fearless criticism of Sihanouk and his cronies. While Samphan comes from a wealthy family, he dresses like a peasant and wears sandals instead of shoes. Unlike my father and his cronies who drive Mercedes, Samphan either rides a bicycle or drives a rusty old blue motor scooter that always sounds as if it will break down any minute. We see him as a patriot and a worthy role model, despite what others may say about him. I was particularly proud of his actions at the restaurant last night."

Hak and I had joined Samphan the night before at the outdoor restaurant in the rear of the Phnom Hotel. We followed Samphan's example in choosing soup and some fruit, while diners at the next table were eating paté and other French delicacies, accompanied by several bottles of French wine. At the end of our meal, Samphan rose, stood before their table and admonished those people, saying, "You should be ashamed of sitting here, enjoying such expensive food and wine, when most people who work ten times harder than you have nothing at all!" We then left before the stunned diners had a chance to react.

One evening Hak and I attended a meeting led by Khieu Samphan and Ieng Thirith, who usually addressed sessions for lower level party officials and leaders of communist youth groups. Khieu Ponnary restricted her appearances to meetings of the Communist Women's Organization, while Saloth Sar and Ieng Sary rarely appeared in public.

During the meeting chaired by Samphan and Thirith, one young man rose to address Samphan, "Are leaders of the Khmer Communist movement leaning toward a peasant-led revolution as in China, or toward a true Marxist worker-led movement as in Russia and Vietnam?"

"Although the Khmer Communist Party is not a party of the working class, you cannot argue that it is not a Marxist Party. We have never been as industrialized as other nations, where oppressed workers form the base of the party structure. Because poor peasants remain the most oppressed class in Cambodian society, this class represents the foundation of the Cambodian communist movement. Ours will be a peasant-led communist revolution based on the precepts of Marx, Lenin, Stalin, and Mao."

Ieng Thirith interjected, "We believe that true communism can best be achieved by One Great Leap Forward, as advocated by Mao Tse Tung."

Another young person rose to ask a question of Thirith and Samphan, "Might it be more judicious to take intermediate steps along the way, before achieving communism all of a sudden, as in one 'great leap'?"

I was shocked to see the look of disgust the two speakers directed at the young student. They smiled condescendingly while Samphan, with an air of superiority, proclaimed proudly, "Cambodia will become the first nation to create a completely communist society without wasting time on intermediate steps. We will accept no more questions on this topic."

****

Hak and I were eager for the day of our wedding, after which we planned to move to a small apartment owned by his family. It overlooked the Central Market and was not far from the home of his parents, with whom Hak's sister Vanny and her husband lived. I was anxious to move into my own home and could not wait to escape from the machinations of my mother and her coterie of women. I no longer had much contact with my father.

We were married in March 1963, on a day deemed auspicious by a Buddhist priest and our two families. The impending marriage was enthusiastically embraced by my mother, who was finally involved in something having to do with my life. At the same time, I knew her real motivation was to use the occasion as an opportunity to display her wealth and influence.

The private ceremony reserved for family and close relatives was held at my parents' home. According to Cambodian tradition, I had ten dress changes for different portions of the ceremony. Early in the morning of the ceremony itself, Hak arrived at my house dressed in a traditional white silk costume with billowing knee-length pants and accompanied by two best men, while a group of friends followed from a distance, banging pots and chanting. As the groom and best men arrived near the house, neighbors and friends showered them with flowers. Then a gong rang, indicating it was time for my parents and me to greet the visitors, after which Hak and I placed garlands around each other's neck. We entered the house carrying a silver tray filled with offerings, including flowers from the areca nut tree, while young girls threw jasmine flowers along our path.

Hak and his best men knelt and paid respects to my parents before offering prayers at a brightly decorated altar. Next, his sister Vanny and other members of his family entered the house, bearing gifts of money on silver trays. In Cambodia, the groom's family offers money to the bride's family—bridewealth—as opposed to the dowry system in other cultures. An official Master of Ceremonies led traditional chants to accompany this presentation of the gifts to the bride's family. Then we exchanged wedding rings.

Finally, it was time for breakfast, with the engaged couple taking turns feeding one another as a mother feeds a child, while the guests looked on. Only after we finished did the others start to eat. After breakfast, we participated in the traditional ceremony in which the hair of the bride and groom is cut, representing a fresh start in their new relationship as husband and wife. Again, following tradition, Hak changed into a red silk costume associated with royalty, and I changed into a dazzling red silk outfit with gold embroidery. After I washed Hak's feet in a large silver tray, the Buddhist priest held our hands together and chanted. In the most memorable part of the ceremony, family members and friends tied our wrists together with red thread and sprinkled water on our hands to solemnize the wedding. All this was marked by well wishes for happiness, good health, success, prosperity, and long-lasting love, accompanied by the loud sound of the gong and the joyful cheers of our guests.

The priest then lit three candles and circulated them among married couples seated close to the bride and groom. Each couple waved their hands over the flame before passing it on to the next couple. While traditional songs were chanted, the candle was circulated seven times and the priest sprinkled flowers on the newlyweds. The wedding day ended with a sumptuous meal later that night, followed by songs and dances. My parents spared no expense to make the whole day memorable and impressive. The next two days involved visits by the wedding entourage to the palace grounds and other public sites, as well as more music and dancing.

Finally, Hak and I were free to begin our new life together. To show my affection for Hak and his family, I, like a growing number of educated Khmer women, adopted the Western custom of assuming my husband's family name. I would henceforth be known as Thoun Sophana rather than Prak Sophana. On our first morning as husband and wife, and on every morning we were together, Hak awakened me by bringing me tea and singing sweet Khmer songs of love.

****

In the seven years between our marriage in 1963 and the end of that decade, time went by quickly as the country went through a time of upheaval and economic distress. Despite the hardships, Hak and I saw our love deepen and intensify. I was relieved to be living apart from my mother and enjoyed living in close proximity to Hak's parents, who treated me like a cherished daughter. After my marriage, my mother became increasingly engrossed in the petty manipulations of her social set, perhaps to make up for the prolonged absences of my father, whom she rarely saw. Whenever I was ill, especially during my four pregnancies, it was Hak's mother who would comfort me, calling me *kaun makk* (mother's child), words that were never spoken by my mother. Whenever I heard those words, I wept with sadness for my own mother's coldness, as well as with joy for the enveloping tenderness of my wonderful mother-in-law.

Before my children came along, I loved spending time with Vanny's daughter who, like her mother and uncle (my husband Hak), would likely be slender and tall. The little girl possessed a delicate elegance all her own, befitting of one bearing the lovely name Jorani (radiant flower). Even as a young child, she had the ethereal presence of the royal court dancers, whose subtle movements with arched backs and backward-flexed fingers represented the epitome of traditional Khmer beauty. Vanny and her husband often talked of Jorani joining the classical dance troupe as she grew older.

As our own children entered our lives between 1964 and 1970, Hak and I selected names for each child based on characteristics they displayed soon after birth. Our first-born was a round-faced baby girl. As we watched her radiant little face the first night she slept in her crib, we named her

Chanmony (moonlight that shines like a diamond). Two years later we welcomed a serious-looking little boy, Kosal (virtuous and clever); and a year later, another boy, a peaceful, smiling child we named Reasmey (ray of sunshine). During my fourth pregnancy, I had become very ill, and the doctor told Hak he feared for my life and that of our child. Toward the end of the ninth month, Hak's mother went to the temple at Wat Phnom, where she made offerings to our city's patron, Yeay Penh, who answers the prayers of women. She had asked my mother to accompany her, but my mother was too involved in one of her weekly card games. After many hours of agony, I gave birth to a healthy little girl who was born just as the sun rose over the city. We named her Arunny (morning sun).

During these early years, I was able to continue at the museum because Hak's mother enthusiastically volunteered to help during the three days each week that I worked. She loved being around her grandchildren, and she and her husband were very generous to both their son and daughter as the country's economy faltered. Hak began teaching law classes in the evening in addition to his daytime classes and acting as an assistant to Khieu Samphan.

The sharp decline in Cambodia's economy began shortly after our marriage, when Sihanouk cut off aid from the United States. Although many of us were happy to see ties severed with the American imperialists whose military presence was expanding in neighboring Vietnam, the Cambodian military was devastated by the loss of American support.

After naming prominent leftists to his government, including Khieu Samphan and Hou Yuon, whose doctoral dissertations in Paris dealt with ways to improve the Cambodian economy, Sihanouk began to implement socialist-leaning measures advocated by these men. These included the nationalization of important sectors of the economy, such as import and export trade, banks, insurance companies, and distilleries. In a speech announcing these new measures, the Prince explained that Cambodia must become self-reliant and dependent solely on its own resources, using wording very similar to the precepts of the new communist movement.

Hak was pleased that many of these ideas were based on a paper he had written for Samphan to present to Sihanouk. At the same time, Hak feared that these new policies would be short-lived. He confided to me, "These reforms will not succeed. They will be sabotaged by those whose livelihood would be damaged if they were fully implemented."

"I'm sure my father and his colleagues at the National Bank will be at the forefront of the opposition. These reforms would remove the source of funding for the all-pervasive corruption affecting all levels of our society."

"You are right, Sophana. Banking, trade, insurance, and other affected sectors will likely remain in the hands of the same old cronies who have always used these institutions as their personal fiefdoms from which to extract wealth."

As Hak predicted, these same cronies persuaded Sihanouk to abandon the new leftist policies—a mistake that only caused more damage to an already weakened economy. As the situation worsened, Sihanouk distanced himself and seemed more and more obsessed with acting and film making than focusing on the government's problems. When asked by a Western journalist to describe his principal job, Sihanouk did not refer to the role of chief of state, but commented, "I am an artist. I was born an artist, and what I like best is cinema [and] music."

While working at the museum, I often heard the curator deploring the extravagant construction projects Sihanouk was undertaking in the city at a time of grave financial instability. Nhem Samchay, my elderly mentor, told me,

Just as Jayavarman VII may well have caused the decline of Angkor through his relentless focus on the construction of new temples, Sihanouk's spending on major projects will likely have a detrimental effect on society today.

I am appalled by Sihanouk's latest addition to the Silver Pagoda on the royal palace grounds. During a recent visit there, I noted that he has placed over five thousand solid silver tiles on the floor of the wooden temple and added Grecian style urns to the temple's veranda. Such waste is unforgiveable! To add insult to injury, the image of the Emerald Buddha in the Silver Pagoda is not even a figure of Khmer antiquity. Made by the French firm Lalique, it sits on a base made of Italian marble. A palace guard proudly showed me another new Buddha containing ninety kilograms of gold and over nine thousand diamonds. These affronts to authentic Khmer art and civilization are appalling! They should be sold off to support the country's economy!

Thinking back on this conversation with Nhem Samchay, I recall a discovery I made recently concerning the curious events at the Silver Pagoda after Pol Pot and his victorious entourage arrived in the city to discuss future strategies for their new government. For unknown reasons, they chose the site of the Silver Pagoda for their two-day deliberations. At night, while others slept on the grounds on cots confiscated from a nearby hospital, Pol Pot placed his cot in the center of the temple, on a raised platform formerly occupied by a statue of the Buddha. Just why Pol Pot chose this site over one with authentic Khmer art and architecture will never be known. In light of subsequent events, it seems only fitting that the courtyard of the Leper King, who took on the suffering of his subjects, did not become the resting place for one who would inflict such torment on the people of Cambodia. At the temple of the Emerald Buddha, the impersonal pieces of European art probably did not disturb the dreams of the sleeping tyrant.

As the economy weakened and the blatant corruption of official people and institutions increased, large numbers of young people abandoned their secondary school and university classes and joined the Khmer Rouge because they saw no future in the cities, except for menial jobs as *cyclo* drivers, waiters, or manual laborers.

One of Hak's duties within the party was to guide aspiring recruits to party cells where they received indoctrination and training before being sent to Khmer Rouge base camps in the countryside. This involved much painstaking effort to be sure recruits were properly vetted, and not spies sent by Sihanouk or his dangerous lackey, Lon Nol. It was not difficult to recruit students, teachers, monks, and urban workers who were tired of the injustices they saw around them and of Sihanouk's disastrous policies and theatrics. This was also the time of the Chinese Cultural Revolution, which inspired many Cambodians eager to overturn the old regime and bring about a more just society.

Hak attended frequent sessions restricted to more senior, experienced comrades, often led by Khieu Samphan. These were usually held in the many ramshackle wood and bamboo houses built on stilts over the swamps southwest of the city, where each house had several entry places from which to escape if needed. To reach these houses, people had to move along shaky bamboo walkways linking together the maze of buildings. Because there were no lights, those unfamiliar with the area had to be guided carefully along the pathways. Hak said that at these meetings, they were encouraged to call each other *Mit* (comrade), rather than *Lok* (Mr.) or *Lok Srei* (Mrs.). They also adopted the western practice of shaking hands and learned to avoid traditional Khmer signs of deference, such as the *som pas*, a form of greeting with the palms together while lifting the hands to the chest and bowing. Comrades were encouraged to forge a new "revolutionary character" and not to think of themselves as individuals, but rather as instruments of the party apparatus known as Angkar. At the time, no one could see this as the beginning of more draconian efforts to dehumanize people.

Party members usually informed each other in person as to the time and place of these closed party sessions. Once, however, Hak received a formal invitation, hand-delivered clandestinely by courier. Curiously, the principal speaker at this event was not identified by name or rank on the invitation. Because of the timing and high security involved, however, Hak surmised that the meeting was arranged in order to present the new leader of the Khmer communist movement. Just weeks earlier, party leader Tou Samouth had disappeared, and Hak wondered if a successor to Samouth might be named soon if, indeed, the elderly leader had died. When Hak returned, we discussed what transpired at the meeting.

"I realize that you cannot divulge all that was discussed, but can you tell me how many were at this special meeting, Hak?"

"About fifty; thirty were monks and the rest mainly teachers and students."

"Was there any discussion of Samouth's disappearance?"

"No, but most of my comrades assume he was killed by Lon Nol's men, although his body has yet to be found and there has been no publicity regarding his disappearance. I would think that if Lon Nol had killed Samouth, the deed would have been openly proclaimed in all the newspapers, with photos to prove it."

"Has anyone within the party structure raised the possibility that Samouth might have been killed by a party rival?"

"Those are exactly my thoughts as well, Sophana, but I cannot imagine who that person might be! The number two man in the party, Nuon Chea, is a wealthy Sino-Khmer head of a large trucking and transport firm who could never succeed Samouth, mainly because of alleged illegal financial dealings and Chea's family relationship to a rural party leader who openly defected to Lon Nol. While many in Paris thought that Ieng Sary would rise in prominence, he is not well-liked by other party officials. His star seems to have dimmed during the last few years, despite his overt ambition. And no one expects Khieu Samphan to assume party leadership, even though he enjoys great popularity among the young and well-educated."

"Now, what more can you tell me about the mysterious speaker? I'm dying of curiosity!"

"First of all, his name was never mentioned, although it was evident that he was indeed the new party leader. After listening to his speech, a monk sitting next to me exclaimed, 'He found words that went straight to your heart and touched every fiber of your being. He was serene, like a monk.' The speaker evoked images carefully chosen to make a powerful impact on his listeners, at this time when many Cambodians are disheartened and suffering from the dire economic situation. He said the Cambodian revolution would return our nation to a level of glory equal to that of the god-kings of Angkor; that Cambodia would become an 'island of purity amid the confusion of the present-day world and a precious model for humanity whose revolutionary virtue will exceed that of all previous revolutionary states, including China.' He concluded by proclaiming that the 'whole world will admire us, sing our praises, learn from us, and follow our example.' He added that one major priority is to preserve the Khmer race forever. This was followed by thunderous applause."

"I must say, Hak, this man knows how to inspire a crowd. Can you describe him further?"

"He wore a clean white short-sleeved shirt and neatly pressed dark blue slacks. He was obviously an ethnic Khmer but had very light skin, possible reflecting some Chinese ancestry. I also noticed that he smiled throughout his presentation."

After Tou Samouth's disappearance, most communist leaders in Phnom Penh remained in hiding, venturing out rarely and only at night. Ponnary and her sister Thirith continued working in order to support their husbands' clandestine political activities. Ponnary continued to teach and retained her position on the editorial staff of Sihanouk's official magazine, *Kambuja*, while her sister Thirith increased her teaching load and gave public lectures on the works of Shakespeare.

****

The next few years were especially challenging for me, with the demands of our growing family and the increasingly dire state of the economy. Everywhere throughout the city of Phnom Penh, from the Central Market stalls to cafés, shops, and other places where people gathered, the main topic of conversation was the precarious economic and political situation. I was disheartened to see many of my husband's students and other educated young people living in desperation on the margins of society. Even though my children were young, I began to wonder what kind of future they would have if there were no major change in government. Throughout the city, more and more people spoke openly about the possibility of a leftist government coming to power and reversing the disastrous policies of our ruling "playboy prince."

Lacking the large influx of American aid that had previously allowed the government to balance its budget, Prince Sihanouk made futile attempts to make up for the shortfall. One of my neighbors, the wife of a military officer, told me that officers as well as soldiers were becoming increasingly disheartened and doubtful of their ability to defend the country now that the conflict in neighboring Vietnam was continuing to escalate. If, as anticipated, the Vietnamese were victorious over the Americans, people feared there might be another attempt by the Vietnamese to invade Cambodia.

We heard through party channels that many members of the military were actually deserting to join the Khmer Rouge forces, as Sihanouk cut the military budget even further to make up for overall budget deficits. Hak and other experienced comrades trained these men in party precepts and sent them into the provinces for lessons in insurgent warfare. While the Khmer Rouge organization enjoyed much success in the 1960s, we also experienced low points of loneliness and rejection. In my own life as well, I experienced the joys of motherhood, mixed with anxiety about what kind of future awaited my children.

In 1963, students in the northwest city of Siem Reap (close to Angkor Wat) staged demonstrations against the *Sangkum,* the political party of Prince Sihanouk. As far as Hak could ascertain, these actions were purely spontaneous and reflected the frustration of young people, especially educated youths unable to find jobs and to survive in an increasingly harsh economic climate.

Assuming that people in the countryside were blindly loyal to a monarch they believed to be divine, Sihanouk and his entourage were shocked to learn of students carrying banners proclaiming "The *Sangkum* is rotten!" and "The *Sangkum* is unjust!"

The party acted quickly to take advantage of the situation. Party cells in Phnom Penh and youth groups such as the Communist Women's Organization organized successful demonstrations in support of the students. We were unaware, however, that this success would eventually lead to a major reorientation of the Khmer communist organization that would leave those of us in Phnom Penh largely isolated.

Sihanouk's lackey, General Lon Nol, published a list of thirty-four people in Phnom Penh whom he branded as communist agitators. Most of those on the list were students, teachers, monks, and some journalists. Among those named were Saloth Sar and Ieng Sary, not necessarily because they were considered to be communists but because they had taught at leftist-leaning schools.

Many party officials decided to leave Phnom Penh as soon as possible and under cover of darkness. Saloth Sar and Ieng Sary fled secretly during the night into the forests, abandoning all major party operations in Phnom Penh. Within two to three days, the entire leadership and organizational apparatus relocated to the countryside. The only leaders who remained in the city were three who had previously been part of Sihanouk's cabinet: Khieu Samphan, Hou Yuon, and Hu Nim.

One occasion when we would normally have been involved in street protests was the August 1966 visit to Cambodia by French President Charles De Gaulle. Hak explained, "This is just a last-ditch effort by Sihanouk to obtain financial assistance from abroad, now that he has broken off relations with the U.S."

"I agree, but I still wish there were some way to express our distaste for the prince's groveling before our former colonial masters."

"I feel the same way, Sophana, but Khieu Samphan and other leading opponents of the regime received threats that they would be imprisoned, tortured, or even killed if any protests marred the visit. I also learned that all anti-De Gaulle French residents have been forcibly removed from the city for the duration of the visit."

"I am so glad that our children are too young to be forced into taking part in the cheerful dances and songs being staged for the event."

We had three children by that time. Our little girl Chanmony was four, our son Kosal was three, and his little brother Reasmey was just ten months old. Vanny's lovely six-year-old daughter Jorani, on the other hand, was to be one of the lead dancers in a special children's program at the Royal Palace. Vanny and her husband had to stand with other parents on the grounds, quite a distance from the open-sided pavilion where the opulent dinner and festivities were to take place.

After the ceremony, the leader of the royal dance troupe approached Jorani's parents and offered a scholarship for the tall, elegant girl who stood out from the other dancers with her skill and ethereal grace. Despite their dislike for the royalty, Vanny and her husband allowed Jorani to join the dance troupe.

After all the pomp and expense incurred for the visit by the French president, the visit did not result in any serious attempt to assist our almost bankrupt nation. Sihanouk was obviously frustrated and undecided about where to turn next for needed assistance. His surprising decision was to turn to our historical enemy: Vietnam. Hak was outraged.

"I don't understand why the Vietnamese communists, who have trained and supported our own communist movement, are now dealing openly with Prince Sihanouk! Khieu Samphan confided to me that in light of this development, party leaders have made the monumental decision to distance themselves from the Vietnamese communists and return to the precepts of independence and self-reliance."

Residents of Phnom Penh soon learned that Sihanouk had allowed the Viet Cong and North Vietnamese to establish base camps in Cambodia and, worse yet, that he authorized clandestine sales of Cambodian rice for them. Lon Nol's military units protected trucks filled with rice moving toward the border with Vietnam. It also became common knowledge that the military was providing security for the movement of Chinese military shipments from the port of Sihanoukville in the southwest to the Ho Chi Minh trail in the north for the Vietnamese war with the Americans. Military officers reportedly charged heavy fees for each truck moving through their respective operational zones. None of this money made it down to poor soldiers who rarely received a regular salary and whose families were starving.

At this same time, farmers and peasants were aware of the huge amounts of money that Cambodian military officers were making through this illicit trade with the Vietnamese. Angry at what they perceived as hypocrisy on the part of the government, farmers in the major rice-growing region of Battambang Province, where Defense Minister Lon Nol had once served as governor, began protests that would end in bloody massacres by Lon Nol's troops.

Just like the earlier student protests in Siem Reap, protests independent of the Khmer communist movement erupted in Battambang. When farmers and peasants distributed pamphlets and organized demonstrations, Lon Nol's troops retaliated savagely. Hundreds of people fled to the forests, where the Khmer Rouge welcomed them and treated them well. While some remained with the Khmer Rouge, others returned to their homes to find them burned to the ground by the military. They also found the remains of protesters who were unable to flee. Soldiers had seized them, tied them down on the ground, and left them exposed to die in the hot sun. To show their hatred for what they had seen upon their return, villagers burned bridges and military barracks. In retaliation, Lon Nol's men captured and killed hundreds of people, poisoned wells, and burned rice stocks. This led many people to decide to go back to the forests where they joined the Khmer Rouge in the hope that a more humane and compassionate form of government led by the Khmer Rouge might soon replace that of Sihanouk and Lon Nol.

Even in Phnom Penh, we witnessed evidence of the violence of Lon Nol's actions in Battambang. On one extremely hot day, I heard shouts and cries rising up from the street, and was almost overcome by a horribly putrid smell of decay. When I looked down from my balcony overlooking the Central Market, I witnessed a gruesome sight and quickly closed the shades to prevent my children from looking out. Beneath our building passed two trucks filled with the severed heads of protesters from Battambang. Lon Nol had ordered his men to send this as evidence to Sihanouk proving that he had suppressed the anti-government uprising.

****

In 1969, Sihanouk opened a casino in Phnom Penh, in addition to others previously opened in the southwest of the country, ostensibly to help the economy. Only a small amount ever made it to the National Treasury, while corrupt officials and dignitaries made huge profits. Sadly, many people gambled away their life savings and found no other way out except suicide. Although I had been estranged from my father for many years, I was shocked to learn that he had lost our home and the family's savings at the casino. He committed suicide by jumping off the Monivong Bridge, a site frequently chosen by those who had lost all hope of recouping their losses.

At the time of my father's death, I was unable to visit my mother because I was recuperating from the particularly difficult birth of our fourth child, Arunny. The day after the suicide, Hak and his mother and sister visited my mother. They found her distraught and unable to cope with the shock of losing everything, especially her social status. She showed no signs of remorse or sadness about the death of an unfaithful husband whom she saw infrequently, but she feared that his spirit was disturbing her peace of mind. While neither she nor I attended the cremation, we each burned incense as a sign of remembrance.

My mother was a Buddhist, but like many Cambodians, she also believed in spirits that make their presence known through physical signs, such as sounds and visual phenomena. After returning from a visit to my mother, Hak told me what he had observed. "She seems to fear that she is being hounded by a *besach*, the demon or the spirit of one who died in a violent or unnatural manner. While I was with her, a shaman arrived to help her deal with the evil spirit."

"What did he do? Did the shaman pray over her?"

"Not exactly, but he gave her an amulet that he prayed over to establish a supernatural link between it and your mother and that he claimed would keep the evil spirit at bay. After the man left, I tried to comfort her and advised her to speak as well to the monk who presided over our wedding. I'll contact him and take your mother to see him."

"Thank you, Hak. I am fortunate to have such a compassionate husband."

The visit to the monk proved to be very beneficial for my mother, whose life changed soon afterwards. I sometimes wonder whether this dramatic reversal was due less to a true change of heart than to a desire to flee from the eyes of women she had dealt with when she enjoyed a life of privilege.

Hak, who accompanied my mother to the visit with the monk, said that the gentle monk reminded her of the Buddhist belief that this life is just one phase in an endless chain of events. An individual goes through many forms of birth and rebirth, both in human and non-human form. What is most important is one's *karma*, the belief that one's future lives depend on one's deeds and misdeeds in this life and previous lives. One can earn good *karma* in this life and ensure a better life in future incarnations by following simple rules of moral conduct, as well as time spent in mindfulness and meditation. After several sessions with the monk, she agreed to travel with him to a temple south of Phnom Penh where she began her life as a Buddhist nun.

Before she left, she came to my home, and for the first time in many years, we truly felt like mother and daughter. We cried and talked all afternoon as she hugged and kissed the children. I noticed, too, that she was still wearing the amulet the shaman had given her after my father's death.

Later that same year, Hak and I went to see my mother. There was no gate at the entrance to the walled enclosure, within which we saw fish ponds, vegetable gardens, and fruit trees tended by local children; also *stupas,* or burial mounds, housing the ashes of monks and nuns who had died there. We walked toward a large hall where the monks taught classes for village children and where both the monks and local villagers took their meals. We were not allowed to enter the sanctuary containing the statues of Buddha and other precious relics, which was reserved for the monks. Beyond the large hall and the kitchen, we were led to the quarters reserved for nuns.

When the monk guiding us announced our names, we noticed my mother coming toward us. Her head and eyebrows were shaved and she wore a simple white robe. She looked more beautiful than I had ever seen her. I also noticed that she was no longer wearing the amulet given to her by the shaman. She seemed at peace and told us that she busied herself with preparing the altars for ceremonies, performing household tasks, and organizing material for the children's classes. She assured us that she had renounced her prior life of social intrigue and power. I never saw her again.

****

Upon returning home from this peaceful visit, Hak received disturbing news in a letter from the Faculty of Law informing him that his position had been terminated, and that there would be no opportunity for him to find another position there. Hak knew that the real reason for his dismissal was his association with Khieu Samphan; all those associated with Khieu Samphan and other leftist leaders eventually lost their jobs.

Khieu Samphan, the man we all revered as the least corrupt official, the one who truly cared about the welfare of the peasants, knew that he had to leave Phnom Penh or be punished by Lon Nol and his henchmen. One night, soon after the demonstrations in Phnom Penh, my husband received word from a courier that Khieu Samphan's mother wanted to speak to him. When Hak arrived at her house around 11:00 pm, he found the elderly woman in tears. Her son had gone out for a walk after dinner and had not returned. She feared that he might have been killed or was being tortured by Lon Nol. Hak could say nothing to assuage her fears.

Samphan, along with two other leftists who formerly belonged to Sihanouk's cabinet, had escaped into the forests where they joined other Khmer Rouge leaders. Most people assumed they had been killed. When party members learned that the three men had in fact escaped safely, Hak immediately sent word to Samphan's mother.

****

Communications between party leaders and the remaining members in Phnom Penh gradually diminished after 1967, to the point where Hak and others still in Phnom Penh wondered if party leaders wanted or needed their help. He confided to me that he received several brief messages from party leaders, emphasizing the importance of uneducated villagers and peasants, as opposed to urban intellectuals and bureaucrats. While we could not understand what this meant for future party activities in the capital, Hak could not dwell too long on these strange directives because he had to find another job to support our family. He learned from a former law school colleague that positions were available at the Phnom Hotel. Not letting me see how much this hurt his pride, he accepted a job as desk clerk in the hotel.

He explained to me later that party members filled many positions at the hotel and its restaurants, which afforded perfect "cover" for transmitting messages to and from party couriers. Thanks to help from Hak's parents and to his job at the hotel, we were able to survive the next few years. As the end of the decade approached, the atmosphere in the city became increasingly oppressive as more and more peasants fleeing from fighting and the lack of food in the provinces poured into the city, which did not have much more to offer than they had found in the countryside. At the same time, residents of the city were becoming fatalistic about the future. They knew the current government was unable to improve the economic situation and were fearful of what sort of future awaited them.

****

Because during the latter months of 1969 we had not received any news regarding Khieu Ponnary, members of the Communist Women's Organization assumed she had joined her husband in the countryside where they were likely preparing for the revolution we hoped would come soon. Despite Ponnary's absence, my colleagues from the organization met regularly in each other's homes to talk about the future and what role we might play once the revolution occurred.

During a meeting at my home, the main topic of conversation was a book everyone in Phnom Penh was reading. *Phut Tumneay,* a collection of Buddhist prophecies, was written in a language and style associated with earlier centuries in our nation's history, although some critics claimed it was a fake. During our discussion of the book, my sister-in-law Vanny described some of the book's contents. "From what I hear, the book predicts that there will be a dark period when cities will be emptied. Another prediction specifies that people will go on killing one another for years until the blood reaches the level of an elephant's stomach. These troubles will reportedly reach Phnom Penh and its vicinity."

Another colleague had written down certain lines from the book, including this prediction, "People will be so hungry that they will run after a dog to fight for a grain of rice stuck to its tail." Another friend said she had read that a "demon king" will appear and will make people think that "wrong is right, black is white, and good is bad."

The dire predictions of *Phut Tumneay* specified that the killings would begin when a comet appeared in the sky and a white dragon appeared in the Mekong. As it happened, a comet did light up the sky for almost a whole week in late 1969, leading some to proclaim, "The Mekong will run with blood!" While most educated people dismissed this talk, it was nonetheless disconcerting. To add to the public's dismay, one of the rare white dolphins that usually stay out of the region near the capital somehow made its way to the banks of the Mekong in Phnom Penh. The majority of people were too ready to believe this to be the white dragon cited in the predictions of *Phut Tumneay*. If we had only known then what fate awaited us in the next five years, we would not have been so dismissive of what we thought was gullibility and superstition.

****

My principal vantage point for watching and listening to events unfolding in Phnom Penh was the apartment where Hak and I had moved after our marriage and where we raised our four children. Our apartment was on the second floor (American third floor) of a five-story white building looking out over one of the city's main landmarks, the Central Market. When Hak first told me that we would be living in this location, I was overjoyed. When I was a little girl, I considered this imposing structure a magical place. I loved to accompany our cook on her shopping days. My mother rarely went to the Central Market, which she considered too large and noisy for one of her social standing.

The focal point of the market, built by the French in the art deco style in 1937, is the large central dome, from which emanate four wings, similar to an "X" formation. I have always imagined that viewed from above, the entire market would look like a huge round spider with four long legs. Viewed from the street, the sides of the yellow sloping dome that rises above the four wings are lined with what at first appear to be steps, but which are actually windows descending from top to bottom, increasing in length as they descend. From the top of each open-air window, lined with horizontal wooden blinds, protrude slanted wood awnings. All this helps to keep out birds as well as the penetrating hot sun. Viewed from the inside, these windows create a filtered light from the top and all sides, lending a cathedral-like atmosphere to the interior space. In addition to the numerous interior stalls for vendors of all kinds, more space was reserved on the outside for umbrella-covered flower and fruit stands, just as we see today.

One could find in the market a wide array of fruits from all over the country, as well as beautiful tropical flowers whose perfume, mixed with odors from the fresh fruit, could sometimes be oppressive under the hot sun. By noon each day, these smells usually wafted up into our apartment. I clearly remember one evening in March 1970 when Hak and I sat out on the balcony trying to analyze the fast-moving events that had recently unfolded.

"Can you imagine a more confusing time, Hak, than these past months following Sihanouk's departure for his annual dietary cure? What a vain and weak creature, having to go to France each year to get rid of the fat he had put on during the previous twelve months!"

"I have heard rumors of a plot being hatched between Lon Nol and Sihanouk's cousin while the prince was away, although I always thought Lon Nol was Sihanouk's most trusted lackey! We all know Sirik Matak to be a puppet of the Americans, but they may have promised him military aid if he could persuade Lon Nol to get rid of Sihanouk. I am deeply concerned about what any future U.S. involvement might mean for our Khmer Rouge forces that finally seem to be gaining the upper hand throughout the countryside."

"I can't imagine that the Americans would send more troops now that they are trying to extricate themselves from Vietnam."

"I wonder why Sihanouk decided not to return home from Paris. Lon Nol announced on the radio that flowers would be planted along the route from the airport to the royal palace to honor Sihanouk's return, but the flowers disappeared."

"A journalist at the hotel said that instead of returning home, the prince went first to Moscow and then to Beijing to meet with communist leaders there."

"This is such a strange and surprising turn of events! Sirik Matak must be livid! Maybe now he will convince Lon Nol to turn against the prince. I wonder what will happen if Sihanouk decides to come back to Phnom Penh? Do you think Lon Nol will have him assassinated?"

"I don't think so, Sophana. Lon Nol will probably prostrate himself before the prince and kiss his feet. He is such a sycophant!"

When it became clear that Sihanouk would not return and was looking to communist allies for help, Lon Nol ordered all legislators to gather outside the National Assembly for an important vote. Hak and I walked toward the Assembly building, which was surrounded by tanks, armored cars, and soldiers with rifles drawn and ready. As Lon Nol's officers ordered legislators to vote for the deposition of Sihanouk, soldiers were told to shoot on the spot anyone not voting in favor of the coup. In less than an hour, Sihanouk was officially removed as head of state.

While most residents of Phnom Penh were relieved at the departure of the playboy prince, their views were not shared by peasants in those parts of the country physically, as well as culturally, separate from the cities, with no roads linking them to the capital. They revered Sihanouk as a god-king and lovingly referred to him as *Samdech Euv*, or Milord Daddy, and saw the coup as a sacrilege.

To express their anger, peasants organized anti-government demonstrations in many areas of the country. In Kampong Cham, peasants killed local officials and emissaries sent by Lon Nol to mediate the conflict. Angry mobs took the livers of their victims to local markets where they had the livers cooked and fed to the crowds. Pro-Sihanouk demonstrators in Battambang killed one of Lon Nol's brothers, cooked his liver, and ate it. There were even rumors of the brother's body having been cannibalized by angry peasants. When similar demonstrations by thousands of peasants occurred at Siem Reap, government forces mowed them down with heavy artillery, tanks, and armored cars.

****

From Beijing, Sihanouk announced that he was now the head of a new Khmer government-in-exile, with Khmer Rouge officials Ieng Sary and Khieu Samphan as two of his deputies. My husband Hak, always a loyal party member, was shocked by this announcement. "I cannot imagine the thoughts of Ieng Sary and Khieu Samphan, who began our movement in order to depose Sihanouk and all that he represented! I do not know how this alignment will affect our cause."

****

After the coup by Lon Nol and Sirik Matak, Khmer Rouge members and officials remaining in Phnom Penh became especially discreet in their actions. Party leaders continued to rely on couriers for fear that the government might monitor other forms of communication. In one mid-1970 message, leaders in the countryside talked of their success in "liberating" (i.e., "capturing") increased amounts of Cambodian territory.

Hak told me of another new party policy delivered to comrades in late 1970 concerning the role of students and intellectuals. While the directive praised their work, which party leaders acknowledged as essential to an eventual victory, it stated that henceforth no more students or intellectuals could join the party. Nor could "middle peasants," those with some form of property or education. Instead, the party was seeking to recruit only the poorest and least educated. After much deliberation, Hak interpreted this to mean that he and other educated supporters would still play an important role in the new society, where they would serve to instruct these uneducated people.

From 1970 to 1972, the atmosphere within Phnom Penh was becoming ever more disquieting. We learned of increasing incursions into southeastern Cambodian territory by American and South Vietnamese forces, supported by U.S. aerial bombardment of suspected North Vietnamese communist sanctuaries on our territory.

Although President Nixon withdrew all American forces from Cambodian soil by June 1970, his government reportedly signed agreements to provide hundreds of millions of dollars in military aid and equipment to the Lon Nol regime. We also saw the beginning of American supply flights landing at the airport and cargo supply convoys moving along the Mekong into Phnom Penh. The Americans acknowledged the widening of their air attacks within Cambodia to include not only the areas bordering Vietnam, but targets deep inside Cambodia. Sometimes we could hear the thundering sound and feel the ground vibrate from bombs dropping outside Phnom Penh.

All the fighting and bombing within the countryside led to increasing numbers of refugees streaming into our once quiet and well-tended avenues and open areas. In fact, between 1970 and 1975, our city grew from a population of 250,000 to approximately 2.5 million. All this occurred while basic supplies and provisions for the city's residents were seriously declining. As government forces repeatedly failed in attempts to reopen major roads leading into the city, especially the roads leading to the rice- and fish-producing areas in the northwest, food shortages in the capital led to levels of violence and looting we had never before experienced.

Around the Central Market area, as in other areas of the city, hundreds and eventually thousands of refugees settled in and created shoddy, foul-smelling slums. Throughout the city, we saw scantily clad, filthy children with outstretched hands, begging for food or money. While I used to love browsing around the market stalls near my home, I now became wary of the poor and disease-ridden newcomers. I no longer took the children into the market area; if I went, I watched my purse carefully. It was disheartening to see the diminishing amounts of rice and other staples available in the market.

It was sad, as well, to see young girls coming into the city to find shelter from the war-torn countryside, only to be forced into prostitution to support themselves and their families. I feared for what awaited my generation and that of my children if this situation lasted much longer. I hoped that our Khmer Rouge revolution would soon put an end to this misery. In the meantime, Vanny and I made several visits to the shrine of Lady Penh and prayed to her to protect our city.

****

In March 1971, one year after the coup, the city was in a heightened state of anxiety. Lon Nol had suffered a stroke in January and gone to Hawaii for treatment. During his two-month absence, government soldiers, who had not been paid for months, terrified neighborhoods by storming into shops and restaurants and taking whatever they wanted. Rumors abounded regarding the demoralization of government forces, which numbered only about thirty-five thousand, hardly enough to fend off any serious Vietnamese invasion.

Upon Lon Nol's return from Hawaii, he was still weak but agreed to form another government. His younger brother Lon Non, who had never served in the military, was raised to the rank of Brigadier General. This was nothing new; in fact, neither Lon Nol nor many other senior officers had ever served in the military.

During 1973, the third year after the coup, we witnessed continued losses by government forces in failed attempts to reopen key arteries leading into the city. January saw the conclusion of the so-called Paris Peace Talks that ended the war in Vietnam. Although U.S. troops and planes left Vietnam, American B-52 bombing of communist targets in Cambodia began in March and continued until August, dropping over forty thousand tons of bombs each month and causing the deaths of at least two hundred thousand people.

I overheard refugees in the Central Market area describing the effect of this heavy bombing on villagers below. They told of people becoming mute while others bled from the eyes and ears, and yet others became disoriented and unable to eat or sleep. Those who survived either went over to the Khmer Rouge or added to the refugee flow into Phnom Penh.

In March of that same year, Lon Nol's men broke up a strike by teachers in Phnom Penh by throwing grenades into the group during a street demonstration. Next, he closed all schools and universities to ward off future actions by leftist agitators. During that year, Khmer Rouge forces cut Phnom Penh off completely from the rice-growing center of Battambang. The ensuing rice shortages, coupled with extremely high food prices, led to food riots in Phnom Penh. I saw previously well-to-do residents taking part in these riots out of fear for their continued ability to feed their families.

Early in 1974, the Khmer Rouge began heavy shelling on the city of Phnom Penh with rockets and 105mm howitzers, causing hundreds of civilian casualties and leaving thousands homeless. These attacks, coming randomly day and night, made residents fearful of leaving their homes. No one ever knew from what direction they were coming, or what the targets were, although many landed in areas crowded with refugees who had fled the so-called liberated zones.

I had supported the Cambodian communist movement since I was a secondary school student and was looking forward to the day when the Khmer Rouge would liberate our entire country. Although I did not share my doubts with Hak, I began to question my allegiance to an organization that would murder innocent civilians and cut us off from needed food supplies.

Early one afternoon, I was having soup in my kitchen with the children and my mother-in-law. Vanny and her daughter Jorani were going to join us later to show us the silver and sapphire ring Vanny had given her daughter for her fourteenth birthday. Before coming to my apartment, they planned to stop in the Central Market and buy some silk of the same sapphire blue color for a dance costume that my mother-in-law planned to make for Jorani. There was one woman in the market who still sold silk produced by Muslim Cham silk weavers whose plants had been forced to close because of the fighting in the countryside.

As we were finishing our soup, there was a terrible crashing sound nearby. The whole apartment trembled, and accompanied by a loud whooshing sound, something crashed through the wall next to the balcony facing the market. Fortunately, we were all in the rear kitchen and not in the living room where the object landed.

An hour later, we dared to move toward the front of the apartment where we looked in horror at a still hot and steaming piece of rock and metal, the size of a large melon, with sharp edges and stabbing blade-like points jutting out from it. In our shock, we could smell smoke and hear screams coming from the market area, where the rocket must have landed before breaking into deadly pieces of shrapnel that slammed into buildings and tore apart bodies.

My mother-in-law and I looked at each other and immediately thought of Vanny and Jorani. Not daring to speak what each of us feared, I told her to stay in the kitchen with the children while I went to look for my dear friend and her daughter. While the structure of the market itself was largely untouched, outdoor stalls were smashed, with debris thrown in all directions. There was blood everywhere and ghoulish sights I cannot even describe—bits of flesh, bone, and body parts flung about randomly.

Through the dust and smoke, I could make out remnants of cloth near the entrance to the market and moved closer to one untouched piece of sapphire blue silk shining in the hot afternoon sun. On top of it lay a slender hand I recognized, wearing a silver and sapphire ring. There was no blood on the lovely hand. I did not dare touch it or try to remove the ring from Jorani's finger. That would have been too difficult, almost sacrilegious. As I staggered back through the rubble and desolation, I saw part of Vanny's face lying among the crushed mangos and melons. I finally lost control and ran screaming toward my apartment.

When my mother-in-law looked at the blood covering my feet and sandals and the hem of my sarong, she knew what had happened. We held each other and cried until I decided to clean off the blood and tend to my children, who were crying as well, even though they did not know what had happened. Later that evening, Hak returned home to learn of our loss. He accompanied his mother back to her home, uncertain of how to explain the tragedy to his aging and increasingly frail father.

****

When we learned on April 12 that Lon Nol had left the country, reportedly with a parting gift of one million dollars from the Americans, we knew a greater change was soon to follow. On April 16, Hak returned home in a joyous mood. His party superiors instructed him to rally young party members in preparation for the impending arrival of the Khmer Rouge into the city. Because of this, he told me, he would stay at the hotel for the next two days. On the night of April 16, which coincided with the Cambodian Lunar New Year, people were shooting guns into the air to celebrate the occasion. I could also hear the ominous sounds of rockets falling on the outskirts of the city.

On the morning of April 17, many cheered as they saw the conquering Khmer Rouge forces enter the city, believing that the corrupt government of Lon Nol was finally over and hoping that the new regime would bring an improvement in their living conditions. That short-lived illusion soon dissipated as an unsmiling silent line of young men and women, dressed in black and wearing "Ho Chi Minh" sandals made of old tires, walked through the streets, seizing cars and motorcycles and shouting at people to leave their homes at once. Those who resisted were shot on the spot. Men with loudspeakers called for government and military officials of all ranks to come to the Interior Ministry and join with them in forming a new government. Trusting that the new regime would not be much different from those that went before, the new Prime Minister and others, including Little Brother Lon Non, stepped forward, only to be executed soon after they reported to the Interior Ministry.

Before noon, two of the young people in black stormed into the apartment and forced us to leave at once to join a column of people walking toward the northwest. We found it hard to understand what they were saying. They kept shouting in a strange dialect and pushing us along, pointing the way ahead of us. I told my children to hold onto one another as we joined thousands of others being forced to keep walking. As we made our way through the city streets, I could hear some people praying to the Buddha while others moaned or cried and kept asking where we were going. The young people in black pointed their weapons at anyone making noise and, with threatening gestures, motioned to them to be quiet. Children and babies kept crying, and those too weak to continue fell to the side of the road.

Within this column of suffering and anxious people, I looked down and noticed the crippled man who used to play the *roneat* (an instrument similar to a xylophone) outside the Café La Taverne. Because he had no legs, he always sat on a piece of wood just large enough to hold him. I never knew how he managed to get to the café but surmised that some kind person must have carried him there each day. Now I saw him writhing on the ground and clawing with his hands, moving along like a wounded salamander. I knew that before long the crazed young men in black would kill him.

After a half hour of marching, we reached the house of Hak's parents. They wanted to wait for their son, but we were forced at gunpoint to keep walking, along with the thousands of others filling the roads leading to what would prove to be an inhospitable and savage land. Throughout what would become a terrifying march into the unknown, people now rarely spoke.

As we were being herded along like cattle and taking one of our rare stops along the road, I met a woman who worked as a maid at the Phnom Hotel. She had rushed ahead in the hopes of finding me. As she tried to catch her breath, she told me, "Your husband Hak and the other male employees, who were wearing their work uniforms of black suits and white shirts, gathered in the rear of the hotel as several wild young people entered the hotel. Hak stepped forward to welcome them and told them he was a colleague of Khieu Samphan, but they seemed not to understand him. They spoke a strange language and looked at everyone with eyes filled with hatred. Suddenly, one of them shot your husband in the face, and another threw his body into the pool. Next, they lined up the others along the edge of the pool and shot them in the back, each falling into the pool where Hak had fallen a few minutes earlier. I was watching from behind the outdoor restaurant facing the pool. I believe these menacing young people thought the uniformed hotel workers were some kind of government functionaries."

Stunned by this news, I walked back toward Hak's parents and the children. Even if we were allowed to talk, I knew I could not find the words to tell them what I had heard, for fear of demoralizing them further. Hak's elderly and frail father, in particular, could not bear learning of his son's fate; nor could my poor children, now fatherless and thrust into an uncertain new world. I had to be strong and maintain a calm facade in order to protect the others. At night, however, I kept imagining the fate that had overtaken my loving husband Hak, who believed to the end that his relationship with Khieu Samphan would ensure his usefulness to the new regime. Hak's main fault was in trusting too much.

During the second day of forced marching, Hak's parents stopped beneath a tree to rest. I tried to get them to stand up again and continue, but Hak's father was too weak, and the men in black were shooting into the air to make everyone move along. My mother-in-law refused to leave her husband's side and remained under the tree with her arm around his shoulders. I kept looking over my shoulder until I lost sight of them. Shortly after, when I heard shots ringing out behind us, I knew what had happened. As the grueling march continued, I saw bodies of many sick, elderly, and weak people who could go no further. The sullen "black crows" either shot their victims or, to avoid wasting ammunition, killed them with blows to the head.

I tried to keep my children distracted and holding on to each other as the march became more difficult. Other children, alone and crying out for their missing parents, wandered aimlessly until being pushed forward by their captors. Women gave birth on the road. While our captors grabbed the babies and threw them into the fields, the mothers often died alone on the sides of the road. At night, we simply fell down where we were, sometimes waking to find we had been lying next to dead bodies.

Our silent column must have walked over two weeks, with little rest and virtually nothing to eat or drink. We finally stopped for two days at a small village where we listened to harangues by mid-level Khmer Rouge leaders. Everyone was searched for any kind of property—watches, jewelry, medicine, radios, or books—and we were told, "Everything is the property of Angkar," the name they used to describe the Khmer Rouge administration and leadership. I did not dare tell them I had been a member of that movement, knowing they would probably not believe me. I also remembered the words of the party directive stating that there would no longer be room for educated people in the organization.

My youngest child, Arunny (morning sun), developed a fever along the way, which worsened as soon as we stopped. She cried out for something to eat, but there was nothing. The other children, themselves weakened by the ordeal, were unable to revive her spirits. By the rising of the sun the next day, she was dead, an ironic end to a brief life that had begun seven years before, just as the sun rose over the city. Before the other children awoke to find out what had happened to their sister, I tried to get some men to help bury her body, but the "black crows" snatched her away from me and threw her into a cart containing the bodies of other dead children. I dared not cry out for I had seen other grieving mothers clubbed to keep them quiet. I will never know where my cherished "morning sun" was buried.

The rainy season began earlier in May than usual, and our forced march became even more difficult as the dirt road changed to mud. More and more, people had to abandon their sandals as we continued on bare feet that slipped on mud mixed with the waste and excrement of people too frightened to control their bodily functions. At one point I stepped on something that caused me to lose my balance; the hand of a newborn baby had been almost buried as thousands of people were rushed along by their captors, oblivious to what was happening all around them.

Once we arrived at our designated work site, soldiers separated adults from children and men from women, and placed everyone in collective work units. In doing so, their goal was to create productive, non-thinking beings who behave less like humans and more like placid animals. We had to remove all our clothing and put on filthy black clothes and black sandals made of old car tires. Adults were forced to work like beasts of burden for over eighteen hours a day. Whenever we seemed to be tiring, young "black crows" yelled out, "You see the ox, comrades. Admire him! He eats when we tell him to eat. When we tell him to pull the plough, he pulls it. He never thinks of his wife or children."

During my three to four years in this system of relentless suffering and horror, where ordinary people became mass murderers and today's executioner could become tomorrow's victim, our captors repeatedly told us, "To keep you is no profit. To destroy you is no loss." I could not imagine what kind of people could now be in control of the Khmer Rouge movement and concluded they must be mentally unstable, sadistic thugs who enjoy persecuting and killing others.

For once, I was glad that I had a stocky build and what my husband had lovingly called peasant feet (large and flat, with splayed toes). I was able to endure more than most of the other women from the city. Those of us who came from towns and cities were referred to as "new people" while the illiterate peasants described as "base people" were in charge of each unit. My earlier choice to dress plainly and wear my hair in the style of Khieu Ponnary made me more acceptable to the base people than most other new people.

Each evening, Khmer Rouge comrades forced us to listen to harangues by local Khmer Rouge leaders about the superiority of Angkar. During several sessions, a local party official read the following directives, which he said were written by comrade Khieu Samphan. Because we listened to these words so often, I am certain this represents the gist of that message:

How do we make a communist revolution? The first thing you do is destroy private property. The method to achieve this is the evacuation of the cities and towns. But emotional private property is even more dangerous. It comprises everything that you think is "yours"—your family, your wife, your children—and everything you describe as "mine." That is why you have been separated: men with men, women with women, children with children, all under the protection of Angkar. Each of us is the child of Angkar, the man of Angkar, the woman of Angkar.

The knowledge you have in your head, your ideas, are mental private property. To become a true revolutionary you must wash your mind clean—clean of the teaching of colonialists and imperialists. It must be destroyed. To make yourselves fit to participate in the communist revolution, you must become like the ordinary people of Cambodia: the peasants. You must wash your minds clean.

When I recalled the idealistic young Khieu Samphan and the empathy he displayed toward the poor and powerless, I could not believe he could be the author of such heartless statements. I concluded that someone else must have written these words. I believed that because they were well-educated people, perhaps he, along with Khieu Ponnary, Ieng Thirith, Saloth Sar, and Ieng Sary had been eliminated by this new peasant-led movement. After a while, we did not hear much about Samphan. The only name the Khmer Rouge comrades mentioned was that of a man named Pol Pot, also known as Brother Number One. All party directives henceforth were attributed to Pol Pot, who was also at times referred to as Angkar, the term generally used for the party administration and leadership as a whole.

The concept of brainwashing and destruction of the personality was encouraged by the new Khmer Rouge leaders, who often made us chant this phrase, "To be a true revolutionary is to have no personality at all." The means to achieve this state was to endure hours of indoctrination and extreme mental and physical pressure.

Each day our captors repeated, "Angkar is always right. Questioning its wisdom is always a mistake." Those of us who came from the cities and towns were singled out for derision and deprived of all creature comforts. We had been uprooted from our homes and abandoned to live in a hostile land where people died of starvation and hunger, women stopped menstruating, others suffered from prolapsed uteruses, and mothers had no milk. Diseases such as malaria wiped out whole villages, while medicines were reserved for our captors. Hunger became a weapon. We were told, "He who does not work does not eat." Those too weak to work were executed. After each day's backbreaking work, we received a bowl of watery soup made from bamboo, banana leaves, and perhaps some rice. Sometimes the soldiers allowed us to forage for snails, spiders, moths, or wild vegetables.

In addition to our captors, there were certain people we sought to avoid, even though they deserved our pity. They were the drivers of the death carts that brought victims to the killing fields each night. While the rest of us were forced each evening to chant violent revolutionary songs played on loudspeakers, the death cart drivers picked up those gathered on the outskirts of the camp and took them to open fields to be slaughtered. There, soldiers handed out picks and shovels and ordered the victims to dig large pits. Next, wild young men clubbed them to death and threw their bodies into the pits. The following night, a new set of victims would have to cover up the dead from the previous night, before being executed and thrown atop those they had just buried.

Those chosen to drive the death carts reeked of death, and people averted their eyes from them out of fear that they might be among their next group of passengers. The drivers themselves lasted in this job no more than two or three months, after which they would also be counted among the unfortunate victims. Everyone lived in fear in this system of paranoia, terror, constant surveillance, and death, where ordinary people were forced to take part in demonic acts.

****

Sometime during my first year in captivity, I learned that my eldest child Chanmony, then thirteen years old, was in the same cooperative as her nine-year-old brother Reasmey. Chanmony, who loved to take care of her ever-smiling younger brother, often saw herself as his second mother. Because they had always been inseparable, I was glad to hear that they were together.

After several months of hard labor building dikes and irrigation canals, which our captors believed would enable Cambodia to triple its rice harvests each year, our local camp director told me that I could visit both children, who were ill with malaria. This was during the height of the rainy season, when flooded areas became breeding grounds for disease-bearing mosquitoes. As soon as I saw the two children, I felt as if my heart had been torn out. Like Arunny before them, they kept crying and begging for food. As little Reasmey died, he whispered, "Don't forget me, Mama." His sister died soon after. Perhaps they were so inseparable that they wanted to die together. At least, thinking that were true, I could console myself somewhat.

I was taken back immediately to my work site, with no time to mourn. Nor could I see where they were buried. Whenever I look at the moon now, I imagine it shining down on the round face of little Chanmony in her crib. Likewise, whenever I gaze into the night sky, I remember the words of the French writer Antoine de St. Exupéry in his lovely book *The Little Prince* that we read at the lycée. When the French pilot of that story looked at the stars twinkling in the sky, it reminded him of the sweet giggling laugh of the little prince who had left this world for his own distant planet. I now try to console myself by imagining that if one could hear the sound made by the twinkling stars, they would be just like the sweet gurgling sounds once made by my smiling babies.

After these losses, I was at the point of exhaustion, wondering how much more hard labor I could endure. My spirits rose, however, when I received word that my son Kosal, who was fourteen years old by then, had found out where I was and received permission to visit me. My joy communicated itself to my worn-out body, which was able to work with greater energy than before. Once Kosal arrived, I could see how tall and erect he was, just like his father. I ran up to greet him, but I did not dare embrace him because we could be punished severely for any display of emotion.

Kosal told me how careful he had to be when visiting me. He said that Khmer Rouge soldiers taught children to act as spies whenever they were allowed to visit their families, and to report any activity that ran against the precepts of the Angkar. He said, "Our work camp leaders tell children that Angkar has the 'eyes of a pineapple' that can see in all directions at once. When one young boy told his group leader he could never turn in his mother for praying to the Buddha or for taking a few extra grains of rice, the leader made him repeat, 'I am not killing my mother. I am killing the enemy.' I will do all I can to protect you, *Makk*, now that we are the only survivors of the family."

I could not bear to part from this intelligent and clever boy, who was so much like his father. Unfortunately, he left the next day and later died far from me, most likely from the virulent form of dysentery that often attacked young people forced into the killing fields. His burial place is unknown, somewhere in one of the mass graves dug for the many victims of the all-seeing Angkar.

****

During what I believed to be the third anniversary of the Khmer Rouge takeover, local party officials said that our entire work camp, which had just completed a major canal-building project, would attend a special celebration at which Pol Pot, Brother Number One, would speak. Despite Angkar's rules forbidding us to gather in groups, many of us found ways to communicate with our fellow victims of this murderous regime, which we learned was carrying out widespread purges of all those within the party apparatus and military who were seen as traitors to the all-seeing Angkar. Everyone feared for his life, even our captors. No one could be trusted.

I was anxious to see the face of this demon named Pol Pot, the man who had caused so much damage to our people and nation. Because we had to stand during the ceremony, I could not see over those in front of me and was too far from the table where Pol Pot and other dignitaries sat. From a distance, I could make out a figure dressed in a neat short-sleeve white shirt and blue pants. He also carried a fan, which I found odd because that is something usually associated with monks. I could see that he was smiling while looking out at the crowd.

Moving slowly and unobtrusively to get a better look, I made my way along the side of the enclosure and almost fainted when the local party leader introduced him. As Pol Pot stepped forward to address the gathering, I saw the face and heard the voice of Saloth Sar! I was so shocked that I stopped breathing and almost fainted.

Trying to regain my composure, I watched closely to make sure I was not mistaken. So many thoughts and questions came rushing in: Where was Khieu Ponnary, Khieu Samphan, Ieng Sary and Ieng Thirith? How and why did the unassuming Saloth Sar take on this terrible new identity? What had happened to turn him into this monster? While pondering all this later that night, I recalled the traditional Khmer belief that all humans are animated by different energies, with some persons having an exceptionally potent, radiant energy that cannot be easily discerned on outward appearances alone. This is the only way I could reconcile the young Saloth Sar with the tyrant known as Pol Pot.

A few minutes later, as I returned to the back of the enclosure, I experienced yet another shock. As I looked around, I noticed Khieu Samphan sitting in a row of chairs reserved for mid- and low-level officials. During his address, Saloth Sar/Pol Pot never acknowledged Samphan's presence, further validating my dear husband Hak's belief that Samphan would serve merely as a figurehead, with no real power within the party organization.

As Pol Pot spoke glowingly of the regime's great progress, I managed to move closer to Samphan. I whispered into his ear that I was the wife of Thoun Hak, his former aide. Samphan lurched back in his seat and turned to me with a look on his face that reminded me of a hunted animal caught in a trap, fearful and afraid of responding to my approach. He turned away abruptly, and I moved away as well, for fear that he would alert the guards standing on all sides of the open-air gathering.

Soon after that disquieting evening, our work camp supervisor summoned me to his office. After greeting me and praising my work, he said he planned to move me to a new assignment. I was apprehensive, wondering if this was some way to test me. Perhaps they were not sure about me, or perhaps Samphan had alerted them to my true identity. I will never know. The supervisor explained, "To destroy the weeds, the roots have to be pulled out. That is, some individuals act against the precepts of Angkar and must be eliminated. Other, more trustworthy people such as you must assist Angkar in uprooting and removing these weeds that endanger the whole system." I knew then that I had been selected as one of the death cart drivers, and there was no doubt that I would eventually become one of the victims.

While trying to decide what to do next, I recalled a meeting of the Communist Women's Organization when Khieu Ponnary asked me to recite one of the precepts of Mao Tse Tung. Unaware of the implications of the words, I had enthusiastically repeated the following maxim: "Either you cooperate with the communist party or you oppose it. The moment you oppose it you become a traitor. Whoever wants to oppose the communist party must be ground into dust." Now I would be taking victims to the killing fields, where I too might one day be ground into dust. Once I digested this thought, I resolved that whatever the risks, I would find a way to escape into Thailand, which I knew was not far from our camp.

****

When I began my new assignment, I was unprepared for the damage it would cause to whatever was left of my sense of self-worth. Almost every night from that time onward, I had to drive my cart and pick up those considered weak or ill, those identified as ethnic Vietnamese or Muslim Chams, or those who went against the precepts of Angkar. There were usually four or five oxcarts and up to five large trucks each night. My cart could hold up to fifteen people. Wild young men, eager to kill, removed all clothing from their victims and assaulted them.

Sometimes they would kill with clubs; at other times they would beat people to death; and for larger groups, the young men fired bullets randomly while group upon group fell on top of those already killed.

I once had to drive twelve older women to the pits, where the crazed young men vied to see who could slit the women's throats the fastest. I had also seen them slit open the stomachs of pregnant women. Before throwing the mothers' bodies into the pits to bleed to death, they took out the fetuses, smoked them over fires, and hung them to dry. Later, they would wear these dried "smoke babies" on their belts as talismans.

Wherever I went during the day, people avoided me. I knew that I had the aura of death about me. I had been a death cart driver for over two months and knew I would not survive much longer. I also knew that Brother Number One was conducting large-scale purges against anyone suspected of being an intellectual. I feared that I might soon be the target of these purges, as did two other women in my group who had studied in the elite French lycées. All three of us had lost everyone we loved. Knowing that we had nothing more to lose, and that we were probably close to the Thai border, we decided to flee. We made our escape on a night when there were torrential monsoon rains and the guards were asleep in the back of a truck under the protection of heavy tarps. Because we were thoroughly familiar with this terrain where we had worked for years building trenches and bridges, and knew the rains would obliterate our tracks, we were able to move stealthily, without detection.

****

After many long, grueling walks at night over treacherous rocky and mountainous terrain, often with nothing to eat, we made our way toward the Thai border. After hiding out one night deep in the forest, we approached a small village where there did not seem to be any Khmer Rouge troops and where kindly residents cooked us rice with a little fish, a true delicacy that made us cry. They also gave us clothes, which were old but far superior to the horrible things we wore, and prepared a package with more rice and a little corn to last until we reached the border. Fearing for their own lives, five of the villagers decided to join us before the Khmer Rouge troops returned. Before we reached Thailand, three of these generous people had died from stepping on mines.

Once we arrived at a refugee camp in Thailand run by international aid workers, it took weeks for me to regain my strength. For the first few weeks, I did something I had not done in almost four years: I cried without ceasing, and no one could console me. I cried for my husband Hak, for my lovely children, for Vanny and Jorani, for those killed during the forced march out of Phnom Penh, for all those whom I drove to the killing fields, and for my battered and bleeding homeland.

I eventually healed and devoted much of my time trying to console and care for the many orphans arriving daily in the refugee camp. Having lost my entire family, I felt especially close to these motherless children.

No one could feel completely safe in these refugee camps. Because there were many Khmer Rouge agents among us, we had to be careful about what we said or to whom we talked. There were also groups of young thugs who had given up hope of ever leaving the camp. To express their frustration and anger, they beat men, raped women, and intimidated the weak merely for their own sadistic pleasure. For that reason, many of the aid workers, especially the women, were afraid to remain in the camp at night. Sometimes Khmer Rouge rockets from inside Cambodia reached our camp as well.

While in that refugee camp, I saw others who had suffered physical torture and pain as well as the loss of loved ones. Some people had become temporarily mute, blind, or deaf from the great trauma they experienced. Even worse, there were those who suffered from a loss of memory. I could see the horror and deep sadness in their eyes, and prayed that one day their good memories at least might return. I had suffered from many unspeakable and inhuman acts of humiliation and pain at the hands of the Khmer Rouge, and had watched and heard others being tortured. Even today, I cannot talk of these terror-filled days. I am able to suppress those memories during the day, but at night, they escape and randomly enter my mind like the bats that fly out of their caves as dusk approaches.

As I watched the western aid workers in the refugee camp and saw their compassion, I gradually changed some of my earlier ideas about them. One American worker, who learned about my education and experience, talked to me about moving to the United States to receive a college education. During the next year and a half, I attended English language classes at the camp and finally was flown to California by the same aid organization that had worked with me in the camp. I found housing thanks to a local Cambodian charitable group and was accepted as a student at the University of California at Berkeley, where I eventually received my Master's degree and Ph.D. and taught Khmer history and culture.

No matter how well I have assimilated into this new life, the terrible shapes of what I had seen under the maniacal rule of Pol Pot appear repeatedly in nightmares. Strange shadows hover over me during the daytime, too, reminding me of horrors I had once witnessed. To confront my fears, I recently decided to accept the position as president of a new university in Cambodia funded by a group of western philanthropists. There, I hope to foster an atmosphere of openness and freedom of speech and to counter efforts by today's rulers—many of whom are former Khmer Rouge commanders—to encourage a type of national amnesia regarding the crimes of the Khmer Rouge.

I also want to contribute in some way toward a much-needed national reconciliation and recognition of the crimes of the Khmer Rouge. I also hope that I may be able to reconnect in some way with the spirits of my dear husband and children, especially if I make offerings at the shrine of Lady Penh and pray to the compassionate Buddha.

****

Over the years, I have sought to gain insights into the metamorphosis of the retiring young Saloth Sar into the demonic Pol Pot, but my research into this enigmatic man revealed nothing definite, except for the influence of his brilliant wife, Khieu Ponnary. Yet, I could not imagine how Ponnary could have been the sole instigator of Pol Pot's murderous behavior. I was finally able to piece together parts of his puzzling personality during a visit to Paris in 2006.

I had been invited to address an international conference on East Asian culture where the principal guest speaker was the Cambodian scholar and philosopher Keng Vannsak. During the 1950s Vannsak had lived in Paris, where he married a French woman who was a noted expert in Asian languages and culture. He also became mentor to many Cambodian students coming to Paris for university studies. Returning to Phnom Penh in the early 1960s, he served as Dean of the Faculty of Arts at Phnom Penh University and renewed his friendship with Saloth Sar and other founders of the Khmer Rouge movement.

While attending the conference in Paris in 2006, I made it a point to seek out Vannsak and tell him of my interest in learning more about the young Saloth Sar. To my great pleasure, Vannsak graciously invited me to have dinner with him and his wife Suzanne the next night. As I approached their apartment door, Suzanne greeted me in the Khmer language. We laughed when we discovered we were wearing almost identical clothes that evening: a black and silver Khmer silk sarong and black jersey top. With her dark coloring and hairstyle, she looked very much like a Cambodian woman.

"Welcome, Dr. Thoun! My husband and I are looking forward to an evening of Khmer culture and food. We have special Khmer delicacies for you, prepared by the owner of our favorite Cambodian restaurant. We will also play some recordings of traditional Khmer folk music for us all to enjoy. And please call me Suzanne!"

"Thank you so much. After several days of lengthy speeches and presentations, this is just what I need! And I much prefer being called Sophana."

Vannsak then joined us, dressed in an elegant grey cashmere sweater, open-neck light blue shirt, and dark slacks, and looking more like a sophisticated European than a Cambodian.

"Professor Vannsak, I must tell you how much my students admire your short stories, poems, dramas, and philosophical writings. You have created a valuable legacy for all who treasure Cambodian literature and thought."

"I am flattered to think that my writing has found an audience even in the United States! I am also very pleased and honored to meet you, Dr. Thoun. I read your biographical sketch in the conference brochure and was deeply moved by your presentation concerning your experiences, first as a supporter and later as a victim of the Khmer Rouge."

"During my time as a member of the Communist Women's Organization, I was impressed with the revolutionary ideals advocated by Khieu Ponnary, and was absolutely stunned when I discovered that her shy young husband, Saloth Sar, had become the leader of the Khmer Rouge. I am hoping you can help me understand how this amazing transformation took place."

Suzanne interjected here, noting that she would have to leave soon after our meal for a meeting at the university, but that her husband and I should remain in order to continue our discussion. Once our delicious dinner was over, he and I retreated to the salon to converse. Vannsak seemed more animated, speaking in the manner of a professor before a group of attentive students. He also addressed me now as Sophana.

"The minute I met Saloth Sar in Paris, I knew this was a young man I could identify with. While Marxist Circle leader Ieng Sary and his colleagues were filled with their own importance and were too doctrinaire for my liking, Sar was easy-going and not at all pretentious."

"How did you two meet?"

"Ieng Sary approached me, telling me of a friend who needed a place to stay because he had failed his exams at a technical school and temporarily lost his stipend from the Cambodian government. In the meantime, he needed a place he could afford with his meager savings, while waiting for the regular stipend to be renewed. Across the street from the apartment where Suzanne and I lived at that time was a café and wine shop, whose owner rented out rooms over the shop. I arranged to meet the young Saloth Sar and showed him the room, which had no furniture except for a bed. I gave him a chair and some kitchen utensils, and when he came down with flu that winter, Suzanne brought him soup and ministered to him.

"I often visited him while he was recuperating. We found we had much in common. After being rejected by a beautiful young woman, Sar had fled Phnom Penh. His depression worsened after his beloved sister was chosen as one of many concubines to the aging king. I informed him that my mother was one of thirty concubines to the previous king, but when she met and fell in love with my father, the old king allowed her to leave the court. Sar and I thus found that we shared a deep-seated hatred of the insidious ways in which the monarchy interfered in the lives of its subjects. We agreed that Cambodia needed a complete change of regime."

"What can you tell me about the relationship between Ieng Sary and Saloth Sar? I could never imagine how Ieng Sary ever took a back seat to Saloth Sar."

"Ieng Sary and other leaders of the Marxist Circle were ambitious, almost to the point of fanaticism. Sary made it clear to everyone that he would one day be in charge of a movement to abolish the monarchy and establish a leftist government in Cambodia. Proud of their academic success and degrees, Marxist Circle leaders did not take Saloth Sar seriously and derided him for his poor grasp of the French language and for studying radio-electronics at a lowly technical school. But even though Ieng Sary had great confidence in himself, most Cambodian students found him boring and difficult to deal with, and began to abandon the Marxist Circle."

"That is interesting. My husband Hak, who joined the Marxist Circle while studying in Paris after Sary had returned to Phnom Penh, heard that Sary's tactics as head of that group were at times overbearing. At the same time, Hak never heard much about Saloth Sar."

"As I saw young Cambodian students leaving the Marxist Circle, I began inviting them and other friends for political discussions in my home. Saloth Sar was a regular participant at these sessions, although he continued attending the Marxist Circle meetings because he considered Ieng Sary a friend, despite the fact that Sary and others usually ignored him. When

Saloth Sar displayed an interest in Stalinism, I sponsored him as a member of the Cambodian wing of the French Communist Party, the PCF. While the Marxist Circle was loosely affiliated with the PCF, French party leaders found its leaders too elitist. The fiercely anti-intellectual French communists saw Sar as a true member of the proletariat because of his attendance at a technical school and his claim to have studied carpentry in Cambodia. I am not sure if Sar ever did so, but the French were impressed with that aspect of his background. Despite his problems with the French language, the PCF chose Sar to write papers and to address other student groups. I could see that Sar was growing more confident in his abilities and gradually began to see himself as a leader, but he kept that hidden behind the facade of the good-natured, affable person he had always been."

"That reminds me, Professor, of a question a foreign journalist asked Pol Pot after he seized power. The journalist wanted to know why Pol Pot had remained inconspicuous during his student days in Paris. He simply replied, 'I did not want to show myself.'"

"I think this represents a bit of bravado on the part of the older Pol Pot. Once the young Saloth Sar started to develop his abilities as a leader in Paris, he probably did not want to appear to challenge Ieng Sary. And he knew none of the Marxist Circle group in Paris would ever take him seriously."

"Because you knew Saloth Sar so well during his time in Paris, what did you think of the now famous article he wrote at that time denouncing the corrupt feudal government in Cambodia, and which he signed not with his own name but with the words *khmer daeum*, the original Khmer? How did Ieng Sary and others react to this rather bold step by a seemingly unassuming young man?"

"People have made too much of this, Sophana. In fact, all Cambodian students who wrote articles for the student publications in Paris avoided signing their names for fear of its getting back to Lon Nol's secret police once they returned to Phnom Penh. Instead, they usually used terms such as the 'Free Khmer' or the 'Worker Khmer'. So Saloth Sar's use of the term 'Original Khmer' did not seem as outrageous as many think today."

"But why did he choose that specific term?"

"He and I had many conversations about the harmful effect over the ages of Cambodia's feudal rulers, who turned their subjects into passive and fatalistic individuals unable to question the authority of leaders they believed to be gods. Over the centuries, the Khmer people were incapable of fending off attacks and annexation by their Vietnamese and Thai neighbors. Sar and I shared the opinion that the Hindu and Buddhist religions further contaminated the original Khmer culture. We often surmised that the original Khmer people—the *khmer daeum*—might have been a much stronger and successful race. I believe Saloth Sar, or Pol Pot, dreamed of returning the Khmer people to this pre-Hindu, pre-Buddhist age of glory by rebuilding the once powerful agricultural economy of medieval Cambodia and eventually reclaiming 'lost territory' from Vietnam and Thailand."

"Looking back at Pol Pot from today's perspective, do you think perhaps that his main fault was in placing more importance on race than on individuals—that his dream to recreate this mythical original race led to a murderous regime and the deaths of over two million of his own people?"

"Unfortunately, I must agree with you, Sophana. Neither I nor anyone who knew Saloth Sar in Paris could have foreseen just how distorted this theory of the 'original Khmer' would become as he strengthened his hold on power. I often have feelings of guilt for having planted some of these ideas in that impressionable young man."

****

After this explanation by Keng Vannsak, I understood more about Pol Pot's dream of creating a new kind of Cambodian people, who would more closely resemble the industrious "original Khmer" who lived centuries before Hindu and Buddhist beliefs and Western thought changed Cambodians into what he considered a passive people. Yet the hideous way in which he went about realizing this dream remains beyond comprehension.

Some have tried to see linkages between the despot known as Pol Pot and his early upbringing. Spending his formative years in the royal court, a Buddhist monastery, and a French-run Catholic school may well explain his need to develop a calm, smiling façade behind which to hide seething feelings of hatred. This same self-defense mechanism may also have allowed him to conceal his desire for revenge after being rejected by a beautiful woman and derided by friends who were more intellectual.

As for his decision to marry the plain but brilliant Khieu Ponnary, it is easy to assume a belief on his part that, unlike a beautiful woman, she would remain faithful to him. Also, unlike other intellectuals, Ponnary could serve as his mentor in a society where women had to restrict their influence to the confines of the home. We will never know if Saloth Sar may also have recognized something of himself in Ponnary's mentally unstable condition.

Others who tried to understand Pol Pot's personality and motivations included Ieng Sary: "Even when he was angry, you could not tell. His face was always smooth. He would smile his unruffled smile as people were taken away and executed." In a similar vein, Sihanouk explained, "He seduced you, speaking softly, always with courtesy."

Heng Samrin, the former Khmer Rouge commander whom the Vietnamese installed as Cambodian Prime Minister after they chased Pol Pot from power, said that Pol Pot "never used the word kill.... He did not seem to be a killer. He seemed kindly. He did not speak very much. He just smiled and smiled.... His words were light, not strong. [He seemed] a kindly, simple person, but his methods were confrontational. He was just a killer."

This is perhaps the most simple explanation for this man who will always remain an unfathomable enigma.

Prince Sihanouk (right) greeting the young Khieu Samphan
during a visit by the prince to Khmer Rouge-controlled territory in
the early 1970s. Photo from a Khmer Rouge propaganda booklet.

This photo was taken by Prince Norodom Sihanouk in February, 1973. Left to right: Pol Pot's wife; Sihanouk's consort, Princess Monique; and the wife of another Khmer Rouge official. Photo from a Khmer Rouge propaganda booklet.

Photo of the courtyard of the National Museum in Phnom Penh.
From *Cambodia: its Land and its People* by Barry Broman.

Statue of the Leper King in the courtyard of the National Museum.
From *Cambodia: its Land and its People* by Barry Broman.

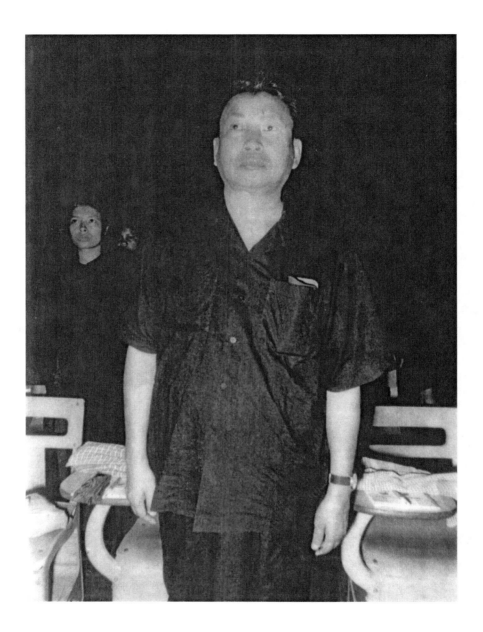

"A stunned Pol Pot entering the torture center at Tuol Sleng for the first time." Photo from Documentation Center of Cambodia (DC/Cam)

"Stilled Lives" depicting a young woman tortured at Tuol Sleng before being sent to the killing fields. Photo from DC/Cam.

A dying baby in a Khmer Rouge camp.
Photo by Barry Broman

Khmer Rouge child soldiers:
Photo by Barry Broman

Previous Page Photo: description

Chinese delegation led by security chief Wang Dongxing arriving in Phnom Penh on November 5, 1978, less than two months before Vietnamese forces would chase Pol Pot from power. Behind and to the right of Pol Pot are Khieu Samphan and Nuon Chea (behind Samphan). Photo from Documentation Center of Cambodia.

Chapter 3

Mother of the Revolution
by Eng Maly

I spent much of my childhood assisting my father in Phnom Penh's Central Market (*Phsar Thmei*), where he prepared mixtures of herbs and other natural material to prevent and treat his patients' illnesses. He had learned this art as a young man in China before he and my mother moved to Cambodia, as did many Chinese in the early decades of the twentieth century in response to Cambodian government overtures to attract educated and skilled Chinese workers and professionals.

After the market closed each day, my father and other Chinese men sat at tables outside the market, nostalgic for the days when most merchants and businessmen in Phnom Penh were either Chinese or Vietnamese (whom they considered as equals). Ever since Cambodians began moving into business and administrative positions under the rule of Norodom Sihanouk, my father and his friends had become increasingly cynical, believing the ethnic Khmer to be lazy and lacking in business sense.

While the Cambodians had succeeded in taking over some trades from the Chinese and Vietnamese, my father's business remained secure. The Chinese had developed their knowledge of medicinal herbs and plants over many centuries and would never consider sharing that treasured science with non-Chinese. Everyone in Phnom Penh had great respect for my father. People of all ranks and social categories came to him rather than visiting the French-run pharmacies. I was proud of my father and his status in the city. My parents insisted that my brother and I receive a good education, perhaps to prepare us to follow in his practice. My brother, however, was never interested in science or medicine, preferring instead to help my mother in the kitchen. He eventually purchased and ran a successful Chinese restaurant in Phnom Penh.

Because he could see that I loved to spend time with him in the market, my father allowed me to work with him after school and on Sundays. I never ceased to be impressed by the huge Central Market with its high vaulted ceilings and immense dome. Louvered blinds created a filtered light that lent an air of magic to the glass counters and stalls where one could find anything, including jewelry, fine fabrics and silks, tools, utensils, and food from throughout the country. Indian women wearing lovely saris and shawls sold beautiful fabrics in a variety of materials and patterns. One of my best friends was the daughter of a Muslim Cham merchant who sold silks made by Cham women who wove the material from the delicate threads of silkworms grown on special mulberry trees on their land in southwestern Cambodia.

But nothing in the market held more fascination for me than my father's own shop. At the back was a long cabinet placed on a heavy waist-high shelf. The cabinet, measuring about two feet high and six feet long, had four layers of small drawers running all along the front. Each of the little drawers had a sign identifying its contents: a dried or pulverized form of a mineral, bone, or plant. On top of this long cabinet was a row of glass jars containing parts of other plants or animals, either in dried or macerated liquor form. We kept a broad array of animal material, either shipped from China or found locally, including bear and snake bile, turtle, rhinoceros horns, tiger bones and claws, geckos, toads, bees, and worms; also, nuts and fruits and hundreds of herbs and plants, such as ginseng and wolfberry. Over the years, I learned the properties and purposes of each of the materials used by my father to cure people's ills.

For example, I learned that Chinese wormwood (*ginghao*) could treat symptoms of malaria, and was an anti-cancer agent as well. One of my favorite things in this fascinating shop was the box containing tiny dried seahorses. I loved the delicate shapes of these creatures used for treating asthma, arthritis, thyroid disorders, heart diseases, and difficulties related to childbirth. Some also believe they are useful as an aphrodisiac.

To determine what formula to create for each individual, my father relied on the beliefs and practices he had learned in China. I loved to listen to his explanations of these practices. "My dear daughter, we are privileged to be the recipients of knowledge developed over millenia by our Chinese forebears. Drawing upon the ancient philosophy of Taoism, Chinese medicine derives from the belief that the human body is like a small universe with sophisticated interconnected systems. In a healthy body, these systems work together in balance, but in an unhealthy body, that balance is upset. The cause of such imbalances can come from the body's own life force or energy (*chi*), from problems in the body's fluids, or from disruptions in one's emotions or spirit."

"But how do you detect these imbalances of energy, Father?"

"I rely on age-old practices of visual observation, smell, listening, asking about the person's life and background, and touch or palpation. I then choose three to twenty-five herbs and other materials to make into a tea or infusion, grind into powder, or blend into tinctures or syrup."

"Isn't that a lot of ingredients?"

"You will learn, Maly, that within each formula, only one or two herbs directly influence the major aspects of the illness. The other materials are designed to treat minor aspects of the problem, to direct the treatment to specific parts of the body, or to help the other herbs and materials work together more efficiently."

In 1960, when my secondary education was completed, I began to work full-time with my father. Because of the fragile political and economic situation in Cambodia, I saw many patients suffering from stress, anxiety, and other mental and emotional problems. I found, however, that I did not have the knowledge or expertise to deal with such illnesses. My father admitted to me that he, too, lacked this specific expertise, but he knew that doctors in China were making important inroads in tackling diseases of the mind.

For my next birthday, my father announced that he had great plans for me. He had arranged for me to go to China to study traditional Chinese medicine with a concentration in the treatment of diseases of the mind. I was proud that my father had such faith in me, and it was with joyful anticipation that I prepared for the trip.

There was another reason I looked forward to this trip. For two years, I had been a member of the Communist Women's Organization whose founder, Khieu Ponnary, often talked about the need for a Khmer communist revolution along the lines of that led by Chairman Mao Tse Tung of China. I wanted to see for myself this exciting new revolutionary movement, which I believed would serve as a model not only for Cambodia but also for the rest of the world.

****

I returned from Beijing in the spring of 1964, just in time for the Cambodian Lunar New Year celebrations. My family marked that event and my return by dining at one of the city's best Chinese restaurants and watching the dragon boat races on the Mekong. We then walked over to the royal palace grounds on the one occasion when the public was allowed to look into an open-sided pavilion where classical Khmer ballet dances were performed, after which the Prince and his entourage drank champagne and sang French songs.

While I enjoyed my experiences in China, I was thrilled to return to work in the Central Market with my father, who wanted to know everything I had seen and learned in China. As I showed him new treatments for mental and emotional illnesses, it seemed as if I were the teacher and he my apprentice. My father treated me as an equal, proudly informing his clients about my studies in Beijing. Shortly after my return to Phnom Penh, a young man named Ly Sokoun, with whom I had attended the Chinese secondary school, began making frequent stops at our stall in the Central Market. As we spent more time together, Sokoun wanted to know what I had learned about Chairman Mao and the communist movement in China.

"I admire Chairman Mao's efforts to create a new kind of society in China. There is such a contrast between the purity of the Chinese revolution and the corruption all around us in Phnom Penh. When I observed the pomposity of the royal court, where they drink champagne and sing French songs while ordinary people can only gaze at them from a distance, it sickened me. I believe the time is ripe for a true people's revolution in Cambodia."

"Now that you have told me this, Maly, I know I can confide in you regarding my own activities. For several years, I have belonged to a clandestine communist cell in Phnom Penh and hope to play a part in bringing about this type of change in Cambodia. I want to learn more from you regarding Chairman Mao's teachings, and perhaps to share this with my cell leader, an impressive young man named Thoun Hak."

I was overjoyed at having found someone who shared the same dreams and hopes for our country as I did, and with whom I wanted to share my life. Within a year, Sokoun and I married, much to the delight of both families. My parents were especially glad that Sokoun's father was Chinese.

****

When a polite young man approached me at the Central Market after I had finished dealing with others needing my help, I could see that he must be either Chinese or Sino-Khmer because of his light skin. When he mentioned that his name was Saloth Sar, I could see how appropriate that name was for him, since *sar* means light or white in Chinese. I was especially impressed that when speaking to either my father or me, he used the Chinese term *Yishi*, which is a polite form of address for a doctor or practitioner of traditional Chinese medicine. I asked him, "Do you speak Chinese, sir?"

"I do not, but I sought out a Chinese speaker in order to use the proper form of address before coming to you for help." I was impressed by this young man's preparation to ensure he used the correct form of address. Sar smiled and seemed such a simple, kindly person that I immediately liked him. He was very concerned about his wife's fragile emotional condition.

"She is the most important person in my life, and the only one I truly trust. She has suffered for many years from anxiety attacks that increased after an operation for uterine cancer left her unable to have children. Although I try to convince her that this does not matter to me, she believes this inability to have a child makes her less of a wife to me. Because she is a very shy and private person, I do not want to bring her here to see you. Could you possibly come to our home, *Yishi* Maly, in order to observe her and prescribe an appropriate treatment for her illness?"

Because this sweet-tempered young man obviously loved his wife deeply, I could not turn down his request. "I must let you know now that I do not believe one visit will suffice. I may need to visit several times a week to make a proper diagnosis."

"Thank you, *Yishi* Maly. I am deeply indebted to you and know you will succeed in helping my wife. I will send our cook to meet you at the market on a day convenient for you. She will guide you to our home."

Before my visit to see Saloth Sar's wife, I mentioned his name to my brother, who was completing his studies at a secondary school, *Chamroeun Vichea,* that catered mainly to those who had failed the exams for entering the more prestigious schools. He told me that Saloth Sar was one of the most popular teachers at his school. "All the students love Sar and find him thoroughly approachable and fair. Although he teaches several subjects, including history and geography, he especially enjoys teaching French poetry. While reciting French poems, he sometimes closes his eyes, as if carried away by the beauty and lyricism of the verses. While this could be laughable in the case of any other teacher, we admire him for his sincerity. He treats us all with respect and dresses like an ordinary citizen, always in a clean short-sleeved white shirt and pressed blue trousers."

My brother paused, then continued, "Students also find it amusing that while Sihanouk founded the school to counter leftist influences among young people, Saloth Sar and other teachers are actually recruiting young people to work against the government."

When she came to meet me for my first visit with Saloth Sar's wife, the cook explained that Sar's wife came from a wealthy family with close ties to the royal palace. She added that Sar and his wife had previously shared a home with her sister and brother-in-law near the palace grounds, but they preferred an area that afforded them greater privacy. When we reached our destination, I saw a home similar to many I had seen in China.

Following Chinese traditional styles, the home faced south, with a gate located at the southwestern corner. Ever since the New Stone Age, Chinese homes have been built on a north-south axis in order to maximize sun exposure and create a sense of security. Today, many Chinese homes are still built facing south, but more for reasons of feng-shui, or harmonizing human existence with the natural energy flow of the surrounding environment.

The brick house was enclosed on all sides by an earthen wall. There was an enclosed courtyard, surrounded on three sides by wings of the single-story house. Here, as in Chinese homes, the rear wing was reserved for greeting guests and more public functions, while one of the side wings housed the bedrooms, and the other, the kitchen. There were no windows on the outside earthen walls of the house, thus providing maximum privacy for those living inside. Just as in Chinese houses, large timbers supported the roof and framed the structure. The tiled roof was gabled, with a single steep incline. While in China the courtyard would have housed a shrine to one of the gods, there was nothing of that nature here.

Once inside, I could see that the house was spotlessly clean. There was not much furniture, just some plain chairs and a low table holding a few books. I also noticed several Chinese prints on the walls. Sar came to greet me, once again using the polite Chinese term *Yishi* when addressing me. I told him how much I admired his home. "It reminds me so much of my days in

China, where homes are built in this same style and the interiors are clean and simple."

"I am especially pleased that you have lived in China. Can you explain to me the significance of the scenes depicted on the Chinese prints hanging on our walls? We were immediately attracted to them when we bought them, but do not know much else about them."

After I told him about the prints, Sar's wife entered the room. I was stunned! His wife was Khieu Ponnary, the founder of the Communist Women's Organization, and the woman whom I considered my mentor! I never would have imagined these two as a married couple, probably because of the obvious age difference. I do not know if Sar had told his wife in advance that I was the person he had chosen to help her or if she had recommended that he seek me out. In any event, she seemed immediately at ease with me as her medical practitioner.

After that first encounter, I spent one or two hours every other day at the home of Ponnary and Sar when they returned from their teaching duties. At other times, they invited my husband and me to share dinner with them. Sar said that he loved all things Chinese, especially the food, since most other types of cooking caused him digestive distress. Once I learned of this, I frequently arranged for my brother to prepare meals for the couple, especially when they entertained larger groups. Sar also asked my brother to instruct his cook in the preparation of Chinese dishes.

When alone with her and during our smaller gatherings, I was able to observe Ponnary closely and could see that she often became anxious and agitated. Even though her husband was usually able to get her to calm down or even to laugh, this was not always possible. Often when I waited for her in the open courtyard, I could overhear Ponnary explaining the details of communist theories to her husband, who listened attentively to his intelligent wife, just as a good student listens to an admired teacher. Whenever other people were present, however, he motioned for her to remain silent. While he respected her intelligence, he was like other Cambodian men, whose wives must limit their influence to the shadows.

****

As Ponnary gradually began the regimen of infusions and other treatments I prescribed for her, she began to show signs of progress, and her anxiety attacks decreased in intensity. Herbal treatments I had learned from my father also alleviated Sar's digestive disorders, as did my brother's cooking. Because he knew my husband and I were strong supporters of the communist cause, Sar sometimes invited us to lectures and party meetings held at his home. I never suspected that these sessions were held there because of Sar's prominence. I assumed he held a relatively low-level position in the party and that his home was selected because it was in a remote area with relatively good security. Party members always had to be on the lookout for the police, who were continually seeking out and cracking down on those suspected of presenting a threat to Sihanouk's regime.

Sokoun and I attended a meeting at the home of Sar and Ponnary, followed by a dinner prepared by my brother. Attendees included Ponnary's sister Thirith and her husband Ieng Sary, the young leftist journalist Khieu Samphan, the gruff Nuon Chea, the prominent scholar Keng Vannsak, and an older man named Tou Samouth, the leader of the communist party organization in Phnom Penh. To these important people Sar announced that he had invited my husband and me because we represented the future of the Khmer communist movement. Ieng Sary, who talked at length with my husband, was so impressed with Sokoun's grasp of communist theory that he later invited him to serve as one of his principal aides.

During the meeting, Sar did not do much talking, preferring instead to listen to the others. When he did speak, however, everyone listened carefully to this man with the smooth face, modulated voice, and calm gestures. After hearing Sar speak, my husband exclaimed to me, "I could easily become this man's lifelong friend!"

After a year of marriage, I became pregnant with twins and saw less of Khieu Ponnary, whose symptoms had gradually abated. When I was about seven months along, Sar asked me to visit Ponnary again. Because I arrived that day before either Sar or Ponnary returned from school, and because I tired easily during my pregnancy, I relaxed in a hammock swung between two trees that shaded the courtyard and soon fell asleep. I was awakened by the sound of Sar and Ponnary quarreling. While she shouted at her husband, I distinctly heard these words: "You must be more forceful and less passive! If I were a man, I would not hesitate! You must remove this obstacle! This is your destiny! You must do it now!"

I had no idea what Ponnary meant, nor what the obstacle to Sar's destiny might be. I just stayed in the hammock, pretending to be asleep. Much later, when the loud voices subsided, Sar came into the courtyard to awaken me. I think he was relieved to see that I was asleep and did not hear his wife's reproaches. "Did you hear Ponnary screaming? She has had a very difficult anxiety attack. Can you help her?"

I had some of her medicine with me and went into the kitchen to prepare the infusion. When I was ready to leave, Sar asked, "Could you please come back tomorrow night? We are hosting an important meeting, which might cause my wife more anxiety. You can spend the night in the side room we usually reserve for special guests. I will arrange for one of the guards to accompany you home."

The next night, I packed a few things and left with my husband for the quiet Chinese-style house of Sar and Ponnary. Sokoun left once I had entered the side room reserved for me. It was an especially hot night, and finding it hard to rest, I moved closer to the courtyard. Here I observed Ponnary greeting the elderly Tou Samouth by bowing in the way one greets a respected elder or a monk. Taking him by the hand, she led him into the central living space.

A half hour later, I heard a crow squawking, and looked toward the front gate where I had heard some movement. I saw a body slump to the ground while two men tied a large rice sack around its torso. Working quickly, the men dragged the body out through the front gate. Although there was no light shining into my room, I was terrified that someone might have seen me, and might want to kill me as well. I moved slowly back to my bed, where I shook with terror.

After I heard other guests arriving, I looked toward the main room and saw Khieu Samphan, Ieng Sary, Ieng Thirith, and Nuon Chea, as well as Sar and Ponnary. Although I had earlier seen Ponnary leading Tou Samouth into the house, he was nowhere to be seen. After dinner, I helped the cook while the hosts and their guests engaged in another of their lengthy political discussions. I returned to my room to sleep but awoke as I heard the guests taking their leave. Looking toward the central living area again, I saw Sar and Ponnary embracing as if celebrating some joyful event.

****

Two months later, I gave birth to twin boys. Both sets of grandparents were thrilled, but my father was the proudest of all. I think he secretly hoped that at least one of my sons would inherit his interest and mine in Chinese medicine and would one day take over the practice. For several weeks, I saw none of my clients, not even Ponnary, whom I greatly respected and knew needed constant attention. Finally, I felt strong enough to take the twins to her home.

Once she saw them, she started to cry. "How I wish I could have had children with Sar! I know our lives might have been very different." She was completely entranced by the babies, holding them and singing softly, even calling each by the words *kaun makk* (mother's child). She made me promise to bring them with me whenever possible.

About that same time, Lon Nol published a list of thirty-four people identified as instigators of anti-government demonstrations. Among those accused were Ieng Sary and Saloth Sar, who left Phnom Penh while their wives stayed behind. This was another very stressful time for Ponnary, but she was remarkably brave and undertook frequent clandestine trips to speak to party officials in the countryside on behalf of her husband. Khieu Ponnary never complained about the difficulties she had to endure; she was completely devoted to the concept of revolution and the need to replace the corrupt regime of Sihanouk and Lon Nol. Although she spoke in a soft, gentle voice, she represented a source of inspiration to party members. She once confided to me that she was a bit envious that her husband was now free to become a full-time revolutionary, while she had to continue leading a double life in Phnom Penh.

Sometimes, when the stress became too much for her, she went into angry tirades against the Vietnamese who were harboring her husband and others in camps located in eastern Cambodia, near the border with Vietnam. Aside from her sister Thirith, I was the only person she could speak to freely. I clearly remember her sharing with me these concerns regarding her husband and the revolution:

> I fear for my husband's health and safety. The Vietnamese do not allow their Cambodian comrades to move away from the base camps. Party colleagues tell me that the Cambodians suffer from living in cramped, primitive quarters where they are prey to illnesses such as dysentery, dengue fever, and malaria.
>
> The Vietnamese are trying to limit the autonomy of their Cambodian comrades. They want us to delay our revolution until after the Vietnamese achieve their victory over the Americans. Sometimes my husband is too passive and unwilling to confront his Vietnamese hosts. I should be there to help him!

****

Ponnary told me in September 1965 that she and her sister planned to visit their husbands at their base camp, and asked if I could accompany her. She offered to have her mother care for my children and those of Thirith during our absence. My husband, who was engaged in sensitive party work for Thirith's husband Ieng Sary, welcomed this offer.

Ponnary, Thirith, and I traveled by bicycle. Once away from the government-controlled area around Phnom Penh, the two sisters and I abandoned our bicycles at a designated location, where a mid-level party leader and three guards took us to a boat to continue on our journey. Moving along the Mekong, a sense of remoteness and isolation descended on us. As the boat wound through wild landscapes where the jungle often reached down to the riverbanks, we saw crocodiles lying on the banks, probably waiting to attack fishermen resting on the shore. We marveled at pelicans nesting nearby while storks and herons flew silently out of the reeds as we passed.

Soon the dense forests were replaced by more open landscapes, where graceful palm trees lined the riverbanks and where we could see men on ox-driven carts moving along the road that ran parallel to the river. Suddenly, we could feel movement in the water and discovered a small group of dolphins popping out of the water, raising their noses and seeming to look right at us. They frequently jumped right up into the air, as if showing off for our amusement. The driver of the boat explained, "These creatures are mammals and not fish. Peasants believe they are half-human because of their round heads and straight mouths. Others believe they contain the spirits of playful children residing for a while in the form of these animals before moving on to their next cycle of rebirth."

"Do you see these graceful creatures each time you travel this way?" Thirith asked.

"No, Madame. It is rare to see these animals this far south. Most freshwater dolphins are found further along the Mekong, as it veers to the east and north. We usually see them swimming back and forth between the Tonle Sap Lake in the northwest and their northern habitats in Kratie and Stung Treng provinces. In the northern provinces, people consider white dolphins to be bad omens."

The driver informed us that we would spend that first night in a village where people would welcome us and prepare an evening meal. As evening approached, the water seemed incandescent, appearing to be on fire in the reflection of a brilliant sunset. As the light decreased, the shadows of trees along the riverbank advanced toward us. It was almost completely dark when we stopped for the night.

It rained all that night and into the next day. Back in the small boat, Ponnary and Thirith took cover under a large plastic tarp, while one of the guards gave me a small umbrella to shield me from the heavy monsoon rains that continued all during the morning. By the afternoon, the rain had stopped. Before we stepped off the boat into the flooded field, the guards gave us packets of ground limestone to rub on our feet and legs. They explained that, during the rainy season, leeches leave the river and move into the fields where unsuspecting travelers quickly find their exposed skin covered in blood. Once protected with the lime, we walked through marshlands where water buffalo watched us as we plodded through the mud trying to keep our balance. Eventually, we reached flat, open fields in which tall sugar palm trees rose up on long spindly trunks, with their delicate branches twirling around the top in ball-like formations. From a distance, they resembled the large round flower heads of onion plants perched on their tall, slender stalks.

After several miles, we came to a dirt road where men walked by us on their way to local markets, carrying long poles on their shoulders. At the end of each pole, they balanced six or eight hollowed out bamboo stalks filled with the sugar and alcohol of the tall palms we had just seen.

Our comrades led us to a small peasant cottage where we could rest for a night before continuing our trip by foot. They waited outside, underneath the one-room cottage built on stilts for protection during floods. During the night, none of us could sleep on our bamboo mats because swarms of ants kept crawling over us, getting into our clothing, eyes, ears, and mouths. To add to our discomfort, giant spiders sometimes fell onto our faces and bodies. By morning, Ponnary was exhausted and under extreme stress. I climbed down to the ground level where the men were waiting and asked them to find some water for tea. I found an old pot in the cottage and managed to start a fire with some branches from under the cottage. Soon I had prepared an infusion to calm Ponnary and help her deal with the hardships we were sure to endure along the next stages of our journey.

That morning we began a four-day trek through more bogs and marshes, which later gave way to deep forests where the guides often had to cut down branches to clear a path for us. In this dark, foreboding atmosphere, it was easy to see why the Khmer peasants believe the forests are filled with spirits. Holding on to rough walking sticks to keep us steady as we struggled along in our rain-soaked clothes, we occasionally reached poor villages where people kindly offered to share their meager meals with us. We were startled by the harsh living conditions of those we met. One woman, who had no teeth and whose skin was crinkled and back bent from years of labor in the rice fields, appeared to be in her seventies. When she told me she was in her early thirties, I was stunned. In remote parts of Cambodia, people had no access to medicine and aged quickly; yet they had no thought of moving to a better location.

At last, we reached our destination, where the forest was so thick and the canopy so dense that it always seemed to be night. This inability to look at the sky or the horizon was especially hard for Khieu Ponnary, but the sight of her husband calmed her. For the first time since we began our journey, she smiled and seemed at ease. After living for long periods in this dark environment, Sar and the others looked extremely pale, and they shielded their eyes from any degree of sunlight. They also seemed undernourished and sickly. I wondered what effect lack of sunlight had on their psychological well-being.

Although living conditions in the camp were rudimentary, the cabins were better than the peasant cottages in which we had slept en route. One evening, Saloth Sar and Ieng Sary chaired a meeting of about twenty party leaders located in the region. The presence of several Vietnamese communist advisors made Ponnary ill at ease. She realized her husband saw the need for continued reliance on the Vietnamese for military support and the training of village- and district-level comrades, but she hoped the Khmer Rouge could soon declare their independence from their neighbors to the east. She was heartened when she listened to Sar address his guests concerning his recent visit to China, "While in China I witnessed the admirable progress made by Mao Tse Tung's Cultural Revolution. Chinese leaders have moved large portions of the population away from the cities to work on the land. They have abolished all titles and rank, and continually purge those considered as class enemies."

Looking straight at the Vietnamese in attendance, Sar read a statement made to him by Chinese Vice Premier and Minister of Defense, Lin Biao: "In order to make a revolution and to fight a people's war and be victorious, it is imperative to adhere to the policy of self-reliance, to rely on the strength of the masses in one's own country, and to prepare...to fight independently, even when all aid is cut off." It was evident from the faces of the Vietnamese that they understood Sar's desire to be free of their involvement. Ponnary later commented that she had feared their Vietnamese guests might try to kill Sar and the others during the night.

By the end of October, the rainy season had ended and we prepared for the trip back to Phnom Penh. Two nights before our departure, villagers invited us to join them in ox carts leading us over newly dried dirt roads down to the banks of a tributary of the Mekong. People were celebrating the end of the rainy season with floating fire displays, in which bamboo frames were floated out into the water and set on fire. As these drifted by the crowds on the shore, villagers drank from large hollowed out coconuts filled with a mixture of sugar palm alcohol and the juice of local fruit. People shouted and sang as the fires gradually died away. Standing apart from the rest of us were Sar and Ponnary, who seemed critical of the festivities.

The trip back to Phnom Penh was much easier now that the floods had receded. Accompanied by two guards, we rode for many miles in ox-driven carts rather than on foot through marshy fields. Once we reached the Mekong, we continued by boat and parted company with our guards after reaching the location outside the capital where we had left our bicycles. We decided to ride back into the city separately to avoid any suspicion. I was the first to arrive in Phnom Penh, probably because I was eager to be reunited with my husband and twin sons. I felt sympathy for Ponnary and Thirith, separated once again from their husbands, who remained in Kampong Cham to devote themselves to the work of the revolution yet to be accomplished.

Once I reached the home of Ponnary's mother, I was anxious to see my little boys. I felt guilty for having been away from them for so long. At age three, each was forming his unique personality, and every week they showed new dimensions of their development. Before leaving for my own home, Ponnary's mother invited me to have a meal with her, while one of her servants took care of the boys. She also asked a servant to prepare a bath for me and arranged to have neatly folded clean clothes placed next to the tub, ready for me to change into before lunch. As I luxuriated in the lovely hot water, I could feel my tired body lose much of the tension that had built up during the difficult trip. Spending time with the older woman provided yet another valuable opportunity to learn more about her daughter and the possible causes of her illness. I included all this in the notes I prepared after the trip in order to reconcile what I had learned in Beijing about mental illness with what I now knew about Ponnary's personal history and symptoms.

****

Once I finally had the energy to compile my notes, I shared my findings with my father. It was wonderful to be working again with him and to return to this cherished site of my childhood where I had learned so much about Chinese medicine. After discussing Ponnary's history and symptoms, we decided on a regimen that improved upon the mixture of herbs and other elements that I had originally prescribed for her.

When I compared Ponnary's symptoms with books and notes I had kept during my medical studies in Beijing, I concluded that she suffered from chronic paranoid schizophrenia. This diagnosis was later confirmed by Chinese specialists who examined Ponnary in Beijing in the early 1980s.

Paranoid schizophrenia usually results from a chemical imbalance in the brain, or perhaps some anomaly in the structure of the brain itself. There are several "risk factors" that could lead to such imbalances or anomalies: prenatal exposure to viral infections, low oxygen levels at birth due to prolonged labor or premature birth, early parental separation, childhood trauma or abuse, stressful pregnancy, and/or stressful life circumstances. While there is a strong hereditary component, this is not always the case.

Although Ponnary's mother had told me that she did not know of any family history of mental disorders, I did not discount that possibility. She did say that she was seriously ill with an infection prior to Ponnary's birth. In addition, the birth was difficult, involving an unusually long period of labor. Ieng

135

Thirith added that when their father left the family to live with his mistress in Battambang, her mother refused to give up the active social life she enjoyed. As a result, Ponnary was responsible for raising her four younger siblings while her mother enjoyed gambling, playing cards with women of her social rank, and attending functions with palace insiders.

Thirith acknowledged that this burden was especially painful for Ponnary, whom all her teachers considered a brilliant student. That she carried out these responsibilities and succeeded in becoming the first Cambodian woman to enter the elite Lycée Sisowath, attest to her intelligence and strength of character. At the same time, this must have placed increased stress on a person of such fragile emotional makeup. Her bout with uterine cancer made her increasingly prone to anxiety and emotional fragility.

There are two other important symptoms of paranoid schizophrenia; namely, social withdrawal and depression. The double life she and her husband had to lead in order to avoid suspicion, and their choice to live apart and venture outside mostly at night, probably exacerbated her propensity for withdrawal and depression.

Other serious symptoms include manifestations of delusions, both of persecution and of grandeur, on the part of a patient with this disease. Such patients often imagine that "others" are trying to harm them. They also see themselves as having unusual powers that no one else has.

While Ponnary did not manifest delusions of persecution with regard to herself, she seemed to "transfer" them to her husband. I recall one incident during our visit to Kampong Cham when we were preparing to have lunch, and someone placed a bowl of soup in front of Saloth Sar. Ponnary abruptly grabbed it and threw it to the ground, screaming and shouting that the Vietnamese were trying to poison her husband. She made the server fill another bowl and have someone else taste it before handing it to her husband. This was only one of many instances when she appeared to lose control and rant against the Vietnamese, whom she believed were out to get her husband. While Cambodians have historically displayed hostility toward their neighbors to the east, the verbal eruptions of Khieu Ponnary were extremely violent and lacking in restraint.

Similarly, while not displaying delusions of grandeur on her own behalf, she seemed to assign a "mystical" aspect to her husband's mission. During some of her non-lucid ramblings, she claimed that he was descended from a superior race of ethnic Khmers known as the *khmer daeum,* or original khmer, who inhabited the wild regions of northern Cambodia during the early Funan period. According to Ponnary, Saloth Sar was the only true representative of this sacred lineage.

****

For the next two years, Khieu Ponnary and her sister made several trips into the countryside, acting as the "eyes and ears" of their husbands and reporting back to them on the progress of the Khmer Rouge movement in various zones. At my insistence, however, Ponnary limited her travel to areas close enough to the capital that it did not tax her compromised emotional make-up. I was able to monitor her frequently, making certain that she was following my prescriptions for stabilizing her condition.

In the wake of violent peasant demonstrations in 1967 against the government's efforts to control rice production and prices, Sihanouk and Lon Nol blamed the events on three prominent leftists who had once served in Sihanouk's government. The three men—Khieu Samphan, Hou Yuon, and Hu Nim—disappeared into the countryside in order to avoid arrest, torture, and probable death sentences. Since most inhabitants of Phnom Penh believed Lon Nol had killed the three men, they became known as the "Three Ghosts."

A few months after the departure of the three men, Ponnary said that her husband had sent word via courier that she should report to an area southwest of Phnom Penh. He also said that he wanted me to accompany her. We would make the trip by car and donkey cart, and the visit would take no more than two weeks.

My husband was in Kampong Cham at that time serving as an aide to Ieng Sary, but my parents were happy to spend two weeks with their grandsons, who were now five years old. One of my sons was especially thrilled at the idea of spending time in the Central Market with his grandfather, peering at the strange and "magical" medicinal herbs and other elements contained in the giant jars and small drawers of his Chinese apothecary shop. My brother loved to bring my other son to his restaurant, where the cooks and servers made a great fuss over him. I thus had no qualms about going on this trip with one of my most interesting patients.

We went to an isolated area about fifty miles southwest of Phnom Penh. Here a fierce-looking, wiry older man known as Ta Mok, who would later prove to be one of Pol Pot's most brutal commanders, was in charge. As we ate a frugal meal of rice and dried fish, Ta Mok said that he had no patience with intellectuals and treated them especially harshly in order to harden them for the tough work of building a revolution. He informed us that the so-called Three Ghosts were now located within his camp.

Ta Mok granted me permission to visit the three men to see if they needed any medical attention. Accompanied by two guards, I found them living in a cramped wooden hut deep in the forest. I recognized Khieu Samphan and the tall, rugged Hou Youn, but I did not immediately recognize Hu Nim, who seemed very frail. Khieu Samphan explained that as they had walked the fifty miles toward their destination, Hu Nim had begun to shake convulsively due to malaria he had contracted en route. At that same time, his hair had turned white, and by the time I saw him, Hu Nim had lost all his hair. All three had skin lesions I was able to treat with ointments I had prepared before we left Phnom Penh.

Hu Nim and Hou Yuon complained to me of their isolation and primitive living conditions. Khieu Samphan, on the other hand, retained an almost dream-like attitude toward the peasants, whom he referred to as "noble savages." One night, after we had finished our meal of fish, rice, and fruit, Khieu Samphan asked Ta Mok for permission to bathe.

Ta Mok acquiesced, and asked two village girls to accompany him to a stream about two miles away. As Samphan and the girls walked away, some of the men shouted crude expletives at Samphan, warning him to behave himself. Privately, Ta Mok acknowledged, "While I consider Khieu Samphan too feminine to be a true revolutionary, I realize the extent to which his image as an incorruptible servant of the people attracts others to the communist cause. Because of Samphan's usefulness to the party, I allow him to take his daily baths, but make him request permission each time."

****

Toward the end of 1967, Khieu Ponnary learned that her husband had moved his base of operations away from the border with Vietnam to the remote mountains in the northeastern Province of Ratanakiri. Because of incursions and bombings by American and South Vietnamese military forces along the border, as well as "search and destroy" operations by Lon Nol's troops against suspected Khmer Rouge elements in that area, the original base camp was no longer safe. Ponnary also learned that Saloth Sar had contracted malaria en route to the new headquarters and had to be carried across the border to a Vietnamese military hospital, where he would be treated with quinine for about a month before returning to Cambodia.

By the spring of 1968, Ponnary decided to travel to Ratanakiri, along with her sister Thirith and Yun Yat, the wife of Son Sen, who would become Defense Minister for the Pol Pot government. Because she knew of the health risks inherent in undertaking such a journey, Ponnary requested that I join her and the other women. My husband had returned to Phnom Penh by that time, and I knew that my sons would have him and our extended family to watch over them.

The three women and I planned to travel once again by bicycle and to meet at an agreed-upon location for the rest of the journey, which would be mainly by boat along the Mekong and its tributaries.

We left prior to the onset of the rainy season. Because of delays, however, we did not reach our final destination until the summer, when the monsoons were at their peak. One of those delays occurred on the third day, after our boat veered toward the west, near the town of Stung Trang and past the red cliffs of

Krauch Chhmar. Because the three women preferred that I sit apart with the boat driver and guards while they talked in private, I was able to observe Ponnary and could see that she was beginning to look feverish.

As her condition seemed to worsen, I asked the boat driver to stop as soon as he deemed possible. In any event, we were approaching dangerous rapids that would have necessitated our stopping and continuing on foot until we passed the rapids. The men pulled the boat onto the shore and set up camp. While the driver took the other women into a nearby village for food, I took out my sack of medicinal elements. After examining Khieu Ponnary, I concluded that she was not suffering from malaria, but from a form of typhus that people often referred to as "jungle fever."

To alleviate her symptoms, I chose a mixture whose main element was the rhizome of the herb known as *Huang Lian*, or Coptis, which is used in a wide range of treatments, including digestive disorders such as dysentery, eye and tooth inflammation, fevers, and sore throats. After the rest of our party arrived with food and material to start a fire, I prepared the infusion, which usually works after a day or two of treatment. After several days, however, her fever refused to abate, and she lost consciousness.

As we encamped at night on mats near the fire, the men took turns standing guard with rifles ready, as we knew there were many types of wild animals in the area. One night we were startled by high-pitched yelps and the roar of what must have been a large animal. The next day, we learned that a tiger had broken into the yard of a villager and eaten the pig caged behind his house.

Two elder women of the village came by on the fifth day, and although none of us could understand their dialect, we knew that they were recommending a way to help lower Ponnary's temperature. Since I have great respect for those who practice non-traditional medicine, I told the rest of our group to be silent while the women looked at the patient. Neither Thirith nor Yun Yat considered me their social equal, but I knew they respected my medical knowledge.

I stood between our group and the two older women and told the guards, "You can shoot me if she dies because of this attempt to cure her fever, but I am confident that these women know what they are doing." I am proud of the fact that I was able to convey a sufficient sense of confidence and strength so that no one interfered with the procedure.

By gesturing toward the men, the elder women made it known that they wanted the patient tied to the body-length strip of bark they had brought. Next, they motioned to the men to tie longer pieces of rope with which to drag Ponnary and her makeshift cot into the water near the rapids. The women helped the men drop Ponnary into the cold water for just a few seconds before quickly bringing her back to shore. Almost immediately, it became evident that this sudden shock to her system resulted in a marked improvement in her condition. Within minutes, she returned to consciousness. Although some of her skin sloughed away and her hair began to turn white, she made a full recovery in about two weeks.

****

My memories of that first trip to Ratanakiri remain vivid today, both for what I saw of this unique part of the country, and for what I learned about Saloth Sar. I marveled at the beauty and variety of the land, as well as of the people, animals, plants, and insects that inhabited it. I felt as if I were visiting some completely alien country, whose characteristics were similar to pictures I had seen of jungles in Africa, Borneo, or the Amazon. As the Mekong entered Kratie Province, white dolphins swam up to the boat, peering in at us. These docile creatures even seemed to enjoy our stroking them and talking to them. Because of their almost human-shaped heads and soft white faces, and their resemblance to dead people or ghosts, I could see why people in the region considered them bad omens.

Once into Stung Treng Province, we encountered dangerous rapids and abandoned the long flat boat in which we were traveling. The driver turned the boat around and steered it back southward with the long pole that he had used to move us along and steer away from dangerous rocks and rapids. Our guards said that we would have to continue on foot for several days until we came to the San River, which would bring us close to our destination. Once we reached the San, we would be met by two mid-level comrades who would accompany us as we rode northward on the river in three small *pirogues*, or canoes.

Before we reached that point, we trekked on foot while the guards carried Ponnary in a hammock tied onto a long pole. She was still weak from her bout with typhus. Much of our travel was over dry red soil that caused red clouds of dust to rise up and cover us as we walked along. Within a week or two, when the monsoon rains began, the soil would turn the water a rust color, and most of this trail would be inundated.

At the San River, we found our guides and one guard waiting for us with three *pirogues*. The more senior of the guides sat with Ponnary in the first boat, while the other man joined Ieng Thirith and Yun Yat in a second boat, and I rode in the third boat with the guard and our provisions. Both the guides and the guard proved to be excellent oarsmen as they maneuvered us along the river.

As we moved further north into this wild area, we noticed the change in the landscape and vegetation, ranging from flat open land to undulating hills, and eventually to the imposing mountains of Ratanakiri Province, whose name is derived from the Khmer words for gem, *ratana,* and mountain, *kiri.* Whenever we stopped to go ashore, we saw waterfalls twenty or thirty meters high, whose drifts of spray drenched us even before we reached the basins below. Several times along the way, the men stood guard as the women in our party bathed in the cool water of the basins at the foot of the falls. These baths had a soothing effect on us, and seemed to calm both the mind and body of Khieu Ponnary.

The gentle people of this area did not adhere to the Buddhist religion of other Cambodians. Rather, they believe that spirits inhabit all aspects of nature, including the forests, rocks, streams, birds, and animals. They are very superstitious. For example, if they hear the cry of an owl or see a black crow prior to setting out on a trip, they see that as a bad omen and cancel the trip.

Each night I had vivid dreams of all the strange and beautiful creatures and scenery I had witnessed. Nothing prepared me for this amazing variety of life, just as nothing prepared me for my meeting with Saloth Sar, who was now using the revolutionary name of Pol Pot. Why Saloth Sar chose this name will never be known. Cambodians traditionally prefer two monosyllabic names that either rhyme or contain the same letters, such as Lon Nol, Son Sen or Yun Yat. It is also possible that Sar wanted to associate himself with the Pol, one of the "original Khmer" tribes living in the northeast of Cambodia, but this is not certain.

The first thing I noticed as we approached the site was that everyone, from the party members to local people living within the encampment, dressed completely in black. They had dyed their clothes using the juice of local *makloeu* berries and they wore what we refer to as Ho Chi Minh sandals made from discarded tires from nearby rubber plantations, with laces cut from old inner tubes.

On the outskirts of the main encampment, there were separate buildings for couriers, for printing presses and supplies, and for the preparation of communal meals. One structure, referred to as a hospital, was run by a few medical students and nurses who had joined the Khmer Rouge to protest the policies of the Lon Nol government. Beyond these were the huts of comrades, followed by the more substantial houses for senior people such as Ieng Sary and Son Sen, whose wife Yun Yat ran and edited the Khmer Rouge newsletter and other propaganda pieces while her husband took charge of military training and indoctrination. During my time in this camp, I noticed that the senior people looked healthier and ate much better than did ordinary party members.

While the rest of our party rested, Ponnary asked me to accompany her as we continued with two guards and a mid-level comrade into an even more densely forested area. The canopy of trees was so thick in places that it seemed as if night had fallen. Periodically, the guards told us to move away while they pointed out deep holes dug out and covered with branches and leaves. Anyone not authorized to enter this area, and thus not aware of the pitfalls, would drop into the holes and die from poisoned arrows planted at the base of each pit. Other types of traps were suspended from tree branches, while guards patrolled in groups of five, carrying bows and more poisoned arrows.

Glimmerings of light through the canopy of trees above us lent an aura of mystery and danger to the surroundings. Suddenly, I could make out a figure sitting about twenty feet from us, his outline illumined by the filtered sun behind him. As we moved closer, I could see a man with closely cropped hair, wearing a short-sleeved white shirt and tan shorts. My initial impression was that I had seen a ghost whose head resembled those of the white dolphins we had observed en route. As my eyes became accustomed to the light, I realized that it was Pol Pot. At that moment, his posture and gesture reminded me of something I had seen before. He was sitting with one leg crossed in front of him while one arm, resting on the raised knee of the other leg, motioned for us to approach. It was then that I realized that his pose was the same as that of the statue of the Leper King in the courtyard of the museum in Phnom Penh. For several minutes, I was unable to move or speak.

I left Ratanakiri in late October 1968, taking leave of Khieu Ponnary, Ieng Thirith, and Yun Yat, who planned to stay with their husbands and continue their work for the revolution. Before my departure, Pol Pot requested my assistance and thanked me for all I had done for Ponnary during the grueling trip.

"Could you prepare some treatment for my digestive problems? I know my wife blames these on efforts by the Vietnamese to poison me, but I have suffered from this problem for many years. I only wish your brother could be here to prepare his wonderful Chinese dishes for me! I would also appreciate some medicinal formula to help me sleep. I often have difficulty sleeping, especially when my wife becomes agitated. I have to move her to our cook's hut when she experiences these episodes."

"My father and I will prepare a formula for you, and I will have it sent to you by courier as quickly as possible."

"Our movement will be forever indebted to you, *Yishi* Maly, for keeping my wife from harm and from the demons that haunt her. Without your assistance and courage, I doubt my wife would be alive today. She truly is the Mother of our Revolution."

Many years later, Pol Pot arranged a public ceremony in Phnom Penh in order to confer on his wife the official title of Mother of the Revolution. Unfortunately, her condition had worsened by then, and her mother and sister had to accept the honor on her behalf.

****

In 1970, after Lon Nol's coup against Sihanouk and the Prince's surprise announcement that he had joined forces with the Khmer Rouge, Ieng Thirith returned to Phnom Penh to visit her mother and children. She informed me that her sister had suffered an acute bout of depression, and asked me to prepare some treatments for her.

I reunited again with Khieu Ponnary in Kampong Thom Province in December 1971, shortly after Lon Nol's failed second attempt to reopen the road to Kampong Thom and regain the ancient capital of Angkor Wat. When I arrived, I met privately with Pol Pot. In his usual calm, smiling way, he confided that he was increasingly concerned about his wife's behavior. "While she may seem normal to you now, she has been displaying more frequent signs of withdrawal, often to the point of obliviousness or inertness. I am also concerned that she shows little interest in eating. Sometimes her episodes of withdrawal are followed by uncontrollable outbursts, usually directed at the Vietnamese."

"Patients suffering from the illness that affects your wife sometimes vacillate between catatonic withdrawal and loud outbursts; I saw such cases while observing patients at the Beijing Psychiatric Hospital. I believe your wife would benefit from a complete examination by experts there; the grueling travels she has undertaken during the past few years have taken a toll on her emotional stability."

"I agree with you, *Yishi* Maly, but I would like to delay any such move until our revolution is achieved. In the meantime, I assure you that I will keep a close watch over her and will restrict her travel as much as possible. Khieu Ponnary is indispensable to our cause. She is the only person I trust to report to me about what is happening in the liberated areas of Cambodia and to identify those senior comrades who are no longer faithful to the revolution and thus need to be purged from the ranks. In order to establish some balance between my wife's responsibility toward the party's needs and her health, I need your support and hope you will be able to spend more time with her in the next few crucial years."

"I am fully committed to the health of Khieu Ponnary and will continue to do what I can, but once the revolution becomes a reality, I will insist that she travel with me to Beijing for a proper diagnosis." Despite his promises to do so once he ousted Lon Nol, Pol Pot did not send his wife to China until the early 1980s, when it was too late to expect any improvement in her condition.

I remained in Kampong Thom for another five months to observe Ponnary. One night she woke me up with shouts that the Vietnamese were coming after her. Other nights she had dreams I now see as strangely prophetic, in which she watched long lines of skeletons marching throughout the Cambodian countryside. As if in a ballet, some of the skeletons stooped over to thrash rice, while others drove picks and hoes into the ground. The parade of skeletons was followed by a march of silent humans with unblinking stares being led to huge pits where robot-like men with clubs sent them to their deaths. At another time, Ponnary awoke in tears, crying out that she had seen a living map of Cambodia trembling and dripping with blood.

I returned home accompanied by two guards and the courier. Along the way, our route roughly paralleled the western side of the Mekong, between the provinces of Kampong Thom and Kratie. One night, as we were resting in a village in a Khmer Rouge-controlled zone, I was awakened by a terrifying noise. Everything began to tremble; the ground shook violently, leading me to believe an unusually large elephant herd or an earthquake was responsible. I ran outside to find others huddled together close to the ground for protection. Once again, the same deafening roar stunned us; we could feel the earth trembling under us. There were explosions all around us.

The sky was lit up by fires, and by what appeared to be huge bolts of lightning. No one dared move or return to their huts. We kept close to each other for comfort in the face of the unearthly fury erupting all around us.

The next morning we met villagers who had escaped from the eye of this terrible storm. Many had dazed expressions and seemed to be in shock, while others had lost their hearing and were bleeding from their eyes and noses. Those who could speak told us that large planes dropping bombs had dug up the countryside, which was now marred with huge craters. Trees were reduced to mere splinters, homes were destroyed, and people and cattle decimated. Hundreds of people had reportedly died during that frightful night.

****

When I returned home in late 1973, I was appalled at the effect tens of thousands of refugees were having on life in Phnom Penh. Slums grew up overnight all over the city, and to make matters worse, soldiers who had not received any pay for months looted and ransacked restaurants and shops. My brother said that soldiers had threatened his restaurant several times, but were driven away by the imposing and fierce-looking Chinese head chef who ran after them, wielding his large chopping knife.

My father was concerned about the possibility of soldiers looting the valuable material stored in the large apothecary cabinet of his stall in the Central Market. In order to protect and secure these valuable supplies, my brother and husband installed a strong iron cage, measured and built to enclose both the long cabinet and the large glass jars arrayed on top of the cabinet. They secured the entire enclosure with heavy bolts and a special lock and key, which my father wore on a chain hidden under his shirt.

My husband and I were concerned about security within the city and worried about our sons' education. There were periodic teacher strikes, one of which became so violent that Lon Nol's men shot at demonstrators and closed secondary schools, universities, and many elementary schools as well. Sokoun and

I knew that our boys were good students; we did not want them to lose their intellectual curiosity and love of learning.

While we pondered what to do for our sons, I was increasingly anxious about my mother's health. My father diagnosed her with a type of cancer that spread quickly throughout her body. While we did all we could to make her comfortable, she did not live to see the end of the year. She was buried in the Chinese cemetery of Choeung Ek, about fifteen kilometers southwest of Phnom Penh. Like all Chinese living in other countries, the eventual goal was to be reinterred one day with their ancestors in their native village. Until that time comes, Chinese immigrants are careful about selecting the site for their preliminary interment. For example, members of the Chinese community of Phnom Penh chose a location in keeping with traditional requirements established in the twelfth century. According to these rules, the burial site must be in an area of fertile land and flowering trees so that the spirits of the dead will be comfortable. The site could never be made into a road or ditch, or be vulnerable to seizure by the high-ranking or powerful. The peaceful Chinese cemetery of Choeung Ek, with its lovely fruit orchards, met all these requirements.

After my mother's funeral, rockets fell randomly into the city at various times of the day and night. Young men without jobs or hope for the future frequently stormed into the Central Market and seized valuables from vendors as well as from my father, who was forced to turn over some of his rarest medicinal substances to these thieves. He began to fear that perhaps he had brought on some of his misfortunes by not having made sufficient offerings at my mother's tomb, and that her spirit was consequently not at rest.

Several months later, Khmer Rouge rocket and mortar attacks into the city grew even more numerous. On one January afternoon, as I was walking toward the Central Market to help my father unlock his shop after the noontime closing, I was knocked to the ground by an enormous explosion emanating from the area of the market. Dust rose up in front of me, making it almost impossible to find my way. Dazed people, choking and crying, moved toward me, and in the distance, I heard people screaming in pain. My first thought was for my father. I was relieved when I saw him sitting on the front step of an apartment building across from the market, next to my friend Sophana's home. I ran up to embrace him since his head was bent down and I assumed he was in shock. I withdrew in horror as I realized my father was dead. At first, I could not understand what had happened since he showed no signs of wounds from flying shrapnel. Upon closer examination, I realized he had died of a heart attack, most likely caused by the shock of the explosion.

I located a *cyclo* driver and gave him the address of my brother's restaurant, along with instructions to return at once to where I was waiting with my father. During that time alone with him, I spoke softly to my father, knowing that his spirit had not yet moved on to the next world. While waiting there with my father, I saw my friend Sophana rushing by, crying, her sarong splattered with blood, but I could not leave my father to go to her aid. I later learned that her sister-in-law and niece were killed in the blast.

Because many residents of Phnom Penh, including those outside the Chinese community, respected my father, his funeral was exceptionally large. Hundreds of people filed by the casket placed under a canopy at the front of the house. Pallbearers later placed the casket in a hearse followed by three cars filled with flowers. Notably, one car contained large sprays of orchids sent from the palace of Lon Nol, whose young aide had regularly visited my father to have special infusions prepared for the General.

Once at the burial site, we poured rice wine onto the ground and placed the white meat of a white rooster and other delicacies from my brother's restaurant in front of the tomb. My sons placed incense, paper money, and paper clothing to ensure their grandfather's spirit would be prepared to join his ancestors. A Taoist priest officiated at the gravesite, reading texts expressing the value of family and the importance of paying homage to the ancestors. He ended the ceremony by reciting a poem written in the 3rd century BC regarding the importance of eventually reinterring the remains in the ancestral land of China. The last verses of that poem follow:

O Soul, go not to the West
Where many perils wait!
O Soul, come back to idleness and peace.
In quietude, enjoy
The lands of Jing and Chu.
There work your will and follow your desire
Till sorrow is forgotten,
And carelessness shall bring you length of days.
O Soul, come back to joys beyond all telling!

After the mourners had left, the hearse waited while my family stayed for a brief rest under the shade of the large gnarled tree under which my parents were buried. I told my sons why their grandparents had chosen this spot, which was actually separated from the rest of the cemetery by a large boulder situated next to the old tree. The graves were placed behind the boulder, facing directly northeast, in the direction of their ancestral homeland. My parents wanted to ensure that their spirits, and eventually their bones, would find their way back home. We hoped that in a few years we would be able to accompany my parents' remains to their final burial place in China.

****

Shortly after my father's burial, party officials notified my husband Sokoun that he would be sent to Beijing, perhaps for two years or more. His official duties would involve serving as a radio technician in the party's propaganda office located in the residence of Prince Sihanouk. As Sokoun confided to me, his secondary role would be to serve as a one of several *chhlop*, or spies, to monitor the activities of the prince. Ieng Sary, who divided his time between Hanoi and Beijing as the *de facto* Khmer Rouge Foreign Minister, feared that Sihanouk might be acting independently of the Khmer Rouge leadership in some of his dealings with foreign officials. Sary needed his own network of trusted aides to monitor and report to him on any suspicious activities by the prince. He knew he could trust Sokoun.

My husband's assignment to Beijing presented us with a solution to our concerns for our sons. We decided as a family that the boys would accompany their father to China, but that I would stay behind. I knew that Pol Pot wanted me to be ready at any time to assist Khieu Ponnary. We stressed to our sons that I would be with them shortly, perhaps within a year. As it was, I would not see them again for almost three years. I was heartsick at the prospect of being separated from my sons, but at the same time, I was relieved that they would be in a safer place and able to continue their education.

After Sokoun and our sons left for China, I busied myself with taking stock of the contents of my father's apothecary, which had escaped serious damage during the rocket attack near the Central Market. I removed the contents from the many small drawers of the large wooden medicine chest, placed them in clean paper bags, and attached tags to identify the contents.

Khieu Ponnary's sister Thirith informed me in mid-1974 that I should move to the Khmer Rouge Special Zone north of Phnom Penh, where I would serve as chief of the medical office for that zone. She said that the office also had a nurse/midwife and two young men who had each completed about two years of medical studies before joining the revolution.

I enjoyed having the company of the young midwife, who appreciated having a colleague with whom she could share her interests and concerns. She had previously worked at the camp of Ta Mok near the Cardamom Mountains, where the cruel Ta Mok threatened to have her killed if any of the wives of senior commanders died during childbirth. He did not express similar interest in the welfare of lesser comrades' wives or of local peasant women.

The Special Zone had its own school, where the children of Ieng Sary and Ieng Thirith received their education. The young people frequently performed dances and songs dealing with revenge and "burning rage." Watching and listening to them troubled me deeply and made me thankful that my children were not subjected to such sentiments. Of course, I kept these thoughts to myself and never mentioned my concerns to anyone, even the nurse whom I had befriended. I knew that anyone, even children, could be serving as spies.

During one of the dances, everyone stood and joined the children as a loudspeaker blasted out revolutionary music.

Men, women, and children shouted and sang in unison the words "Blood avenges blood! Blood avenges blood!" Whenever they pronounced the word "blood," people pounded their chests with clenched fists; at the word "avenge," they brought their arms out straight, once again with clenched fists rather than open hands. One song that became a sort of "national anthem" of the revolution was entitled "The Red Flag." It contained more such references to violence, vengeance, and anger toward enemies. People sang this at the beginning of the day and again in the evening. The words are as follows:

Glittering red blood blankets the earth—
Blood given up to liberate the people:
Blood of workers, peasants and intellectuals;
Blood of young men, Buddhist monks, and girls.
The blood swirls away, and flows upward, gently, into
          the sky,
Turning into a red, revolutionary flag.
Red flag! Red flag! Flying now! Flying now!
O beloved friends, pursue, strike and hit the enemy.
Red flag! Red flag! Flying now!
Don't leave a single reactionary imperialist alive!
Seething with anger, let us wipe out all enemies of
          Kampuchea.
Let us strike and take victory! Victory! Victory!

There was one person within the Special Zone who inspired fear in everyone. Some referred to him privately as the King of Death, since he alone decided who would live or die. This man, a short, spindly former school teacher, presided over all interrogations of those considered traitors of the revolution. Known by the revolutionary name Duch, Kaing Guek Eav was the chief of the *Santebal,* a special security unit. I never spoke directly with him, but in observing his dealings with others, I found him to be ill tempered, impatient, and doctrinaire. His chief deputy Chan Mam Nay, known as Chan, was also a former teacher. Tall and thin, his pockmarked face added to the revulsion many felt toward him.

Soon after the Khmer Rouge victory, Duch moved the *Santebal* operation to Phnom Penh where it became the main vehicle for Khmer Rouge purges. The new prison, known by the code name S-21, was located in a former high school at Tuol Sleng. After torture and interrogations at Tuol Sleng, victims were sent to a special killing field located south of the city.

In mid-March 1975, there was unusual activity in the Special Zone. We were told that Brother Number One would soon be arriving in the Special Zone in preparation for the final assault on Phnom Penh and the victorious establishment of a new government known as Democratic Kampuchea. I was relieved that the period of waiting would at last be over and that our lives could return to some degree of normalcy. Before Pol Pot arrived, a truck came to take me to the leadership's base camp in the eastern foothills of the Cardamom Mountains.

I recognized the route to the Cardamoms from my previous trip to Ta Mok's camp with Khieu Ponnary. I was familiar with the dense forests and narrow passageways as we moved along what had been the Royal Road between the former royal capital of Oudong and Pursat in the north. The encampment, where Khieu Ponnary was located, was about thirty miles northwest of Phnom Penh. A few miles further, in the foothills, was the fortified camp of Ta Mok, surrounded by bunkers and trenches dug in 1973 as protection against the heavy American B-52 bombing of the area. I found Ponnary reclining in a hammock beneath ancient mango trees. She seemed happy to see me and immediately asked about my sons. I was to stay with Ponnary until we received word that she should join her husband in Phnom Penh.

About one month later, we received word that victory had been achieved. While there were no celebrations, everyone seemed excited about the end to the corrupt rule of Lon Nol. We were informed in late May that Brother Number One had already entered the city of Phnom Penh, where he was meeting with key leaders at the Silver Pagoda to map out the policies for the new government. A courier informed us that Ponnary could now move to Phnom Penh.

Along the way, we stopped at what was the operational control center for the final Khmer Rouge assault, under the leadership of Son Sen who was in charge of defense and security matters. Located along the abandoned rail line between Phnom Penh and Battambang, the center was unlike anything I had ever seen. The area contained dozens of grass-covered mounds, each about twenty feet tall, which were actually huge anthills with trees and clumps of bamboo growing out of them. We were taken on a tour of the trenches and underground tunnels that ran between the anthills and extended into holes dug into the anthills, where offices and sleeping areas were located. Both the openings in the anthills and the underground trenches were lined with wood and rice husks to absorb shocks from the American bombing campaign.

All along our route into Phnom Penh, we saw abandoned carts and packages left behind by the thousands of people who had been forcibly marched out of the city the month before. I was stunned to see that the city of Phnom Penh had become a ghost town. There were just a few people in streets filled with the debris of burned vehicles and belongings of those forced to flee. Every building and residence had been ransacked. I saw a few scrawny dogs foraging in the streets, along with pigs, chickens, and other farm animals brought by peasants who had never been in a city before and were now taking over the homes of those who had fled.

As I began to grasp the enormity of what had occurred in the city, whose entire population had been evacuated, I felt a terrible sense of sadness and loss, especially when I thought about my brother. I wondered how I would ever find where he had been taken, in what must have been a chaotic exodus. As we drove by the building where his restaurant was located, I could see nothing but broken windows and tables strewn about the sidewalk. My memory kept returning to the day we buried our father. I hoped my brother would one day come with me to gather our parents' bones for final burial in their homeland of China, where their spirits would at last achieve peace.

Our driver eventually brought us to a more prosperous-looking section of the city where senior Khmer Rouge leaders were based. We arrived at the home of Ieng Thirith and her husband Ieng Sary, who had recently come from Beijing to attend the planning meetings at the Silver Pagoda. He told me that my husband and sons were doing well, and that the boys were excelling at school and mastering both Chinese and English.

I could see that Khieu Ponnary, the true revolutionary of her family, was uneasy surrounded by the wealth and luxury of her sister's home. She was anxious to get to the smaller house prepared for her, where I would also stay in order to monitor her fragile mental state. That evening, her husband arrived and joined us for a dinner prepared by the woman who would act as cook and maid for Ponnary whenever she was in Phnom Penh. He left after an hour, explaining that he never stayed in the same place for more than two consecutive nights. Although we saw him rarely during the first few months of the new regime, we knew that he was deeply involved in the creation of policies and structures for the new communist government.

During the next months, many people came to me for medical advice, since there were no real doctors at local hospitals to help them. Without sufficient supplies, however, my assistance was minimal. After much apprehension, I finally summoned the strength to visit the Central Market where my father's apothecary was located. Although it had survived the rocket attacks of the previous year, nothing remained of the beautiful wooden cabinet whose many tiny drawers held such fascination for me as a child. The iron fence covering the cabinet was gone, and the only sign of the cabinet that once stood behind it was a small pile of broken wood, the rest of which had most likely become firewood.

For the first time in many years, uncontrollable sobbing, caused by mourning for my parents and for this city whose beauty had been defiled, seized me. Unease with the new regime was beginning to grow within me. While I would continue to serve the revolution that I still believed in, I felt uncomfortable with the idea of forced evacuations from the cities and uncertain about the future direction of the new regime.

****

In early 1976, I made my last trip with Ponnary. She wanted to visit the northwest city of Battambang in order to assess the strength and weaknesses of the new regime in that area. We rode in a large American car that moved at high speeds through the countryside. One group of peasants bowed down and greeted us with hands folded over their heads, crying out *Samdech Euv* (Milord Daddy), the name they used for Prince Sihanouk, who had often travelled to the countryside in a similar vehicle. They must have believed their revered prince had returned, perhaps to save them from the brutal existence they now experienced.

When we approached what appeared to be a senior Khmer Rouge official, Ponnary asked the driver to stop. She directed the official to the location where the peasants had cried out the name of Sihanouk. I knew those peasants would soon be dead since any sign of respect for Sihanouk, even the mention of his name or hanging pictures of him in one's home, could be cause for execution.

After lunch with the local party leaders, one of them escorted us to the limestone caves, which they proudly described as "key to purifying the party of undesirable elements." The landscape over which we travelled was flat, except for the limestone hills rising to about 300 kilometers above the plain. The local official told us that this same terrain extended westward toward the gem-mining area of Pailin, near the Thai border. He added that the openings on top of the hills were generally too small, but one of these, known as Phnom Sampeu, contained several caves of particular value.

We reached Phnom Sampeu after about an hour's drive and could see a small temple atop the hill. Once we climbed to the top, the official said the Khmer Rouge used this temple to deal with those who defied the precepts of the all-seeing Angkar. While the official offered no further explanation, we could see piles of bloodied clothing and electric wires used for torture. The official proudly noted that guilty parties were tortured, blindfolded, and led to the caves, where they were pushed over the edge, eventually falling on top of other bodies in various stages of decay. Those awaiting their turn could hear the screams of victims being thrown into these holes, where they would die either from the fall itself or from starvation and dehydration as more bodies were dumped on top of them. I could not believe what I was hearing from this man who spoke in a monotone, as if he were describing some type of harmless mechanical procedure.

Khieu Ponnary responded in the same hollow tone. She stressed that the party must be purified of all undesirable elements, especially those formerly associated with the regimes of Sihanouk or Lon Nol. Throughout this time, I felt suffocated by the heat and pervasive stench of death and decay, and by the offensive nature of this conversation between Ponnary and the local official.

Back in the official's office inside one of the caves, I noticed that the ceilings were covered with strange blackened forms hanging along the walls. Some of the guards also wore these objects hanging from their belts. The officer explained that wives of former Lon Nol soldiers or other women considered a threat to the revolution had to be eliminated, even if they were pregnant. Such women would be taken to the temple we had earlier seen and tied to chains along the walls, where their stomachs were slit open while they were still alive. As the blood drained away from the dying women, it was washed away through pipes leading away from the temple. At the same time, the fetuses would be taken from the mother's bodies and string tied around their necks to strangle them. Next, they were dried over open flames. The dried, black, and shrunken forms we had seen along the walls and on the belts of the men, referred to as *kaun krak*, or smoke babies, were treated as talismans or simply as souvenirs of the war against imperialism.

Although Ponnary did not react at that time to this sordid and hideous sight, she told the official in charge that she was tired and wanted to return to the residence where we planned to rest before returning to Phnom Penh the next day. She kept silent throughout the return to Battambang. Before she went to sleep that night, I gave her some medication to calm her spirits.

After about one or two hours, she began sleepwalking and screaming out "*kaun makk, kaun makk,*" the term of endearment used by Khmer mothers to speak to their babies. She was crying out to babies that only she could see and hear, "I am not to blame! Please leave me alone!" I knew how much Ponnary loved children and that the scene we had witnessed in the caves must have triggered a severe return of her emotional illness. For days and months afterward, this same nightmare would awaken her, while she fled from the pursuing smoke babies, who probably haunted her for the rest of her days.

****

A few months after that trip to Battambang, I received a message from Ieng Thirith, whose husband had just returned from Beijing. Thirith said that her husband had arranged for me to move to Beijing to be with my family. She added that nothing more could be done to help Ponnary, who seemed beyond any possibility of improvement. I had spent so many years with Ponnary that I felt deep sadness at having to leave her, knowing that she was on a rapid descent into full madness. I knew I had done more for her than perhaps anyone else could, but my over-riding emotion was of relief and joy at reuniting with my husband and sons.

Before I left for Beijing, Pol Pot came to thank me for my devotion to his wife. He had a special request which he stressed must be kept in complete confidentiality. "While my poor wife believes the Vietnamese are out to get me, I am concerned not just about the Vietnamese threat, but also any possible efforts by Americans or Russians to engineer some kind of takeover. If that happens, I greatly fear being taken prisoner or worse, being assassinated. To preclude such a possibility, could you prepare a poison that would act quickly and quietly if the need arises? It should be made into a powdered form so that it can be preserved longer, perhaps for several years."

"The material I need is not available in this country, but I can have the appropriate mixture prepared in Beijing and have it flown by special courier, to be delivered personally and opened by you alone." He thanked me and left abruptly, after embracing his wife who smiled vaguely, as if she did not quite recognize him.

After invading Vietnamese troops chased Pol Pot from power in 1979, I returned to Phnom Penh with my husband and sons. I learned then that Ponnary had lost all touch with reality and was staying in Pailin with her sister's family. In 1996, she joined Ieng Sary and his family, who moved back to Phnom Penh under a royal pardon from Sihanouk for a conviction of genocide handed down by a Vietnamese-sponsored court in 1979. Once back in Phnom Penh, Ieng Sary built a palatial three-story villa in a gracious old part of the city.

I visited this home once to see Ponnary, who surprised me by recognizing me immediately. She asked about her husband, wanting to know about his health and if he was able to sleep. Every question she asked was about him. I dared not tell her that he had remarried and had a daughter with the young peasant woman he had selected at random as his wife. After a few moments, Ponnary resumed a blank expression and stared beyond me, unaware of my presence. Khieu Ponnary died in 2003 at age 83, unaware that five years earlier, her husband had died in a remote mountainous area near the Thai border (possibly from the poison I had once prepared for him).

****

Upon our return to Phnom Penh in the early 1980s, my husband and I met many people who had been evacuated from the city in 1975 but finally made their way back to the capital. Most were beyond recognition, wearing the same blank expression and trying not to make direct eye contact with others. They had lived in fear for so long that they found it hard to trust anyone.

Unlike Ieng Sary, Khieu Samphan, and other leaders who had gained weight by eating expensive food cooked by private chefs, those returning from the horrors of the killing fields resembled skeletons. One of those who eventually made his way back was my brother, whom I could not recognize at first; but when he mentioned the names of our parents and described my father's shop in the Central Market, I embraced him at once and took him home to prepare a nutritious meal for him.

For several days, he could not speak of the horrors he had witnessed, but he gradually began to dredge up those painful memories and to share them with Sokoun and me. As he spoke,

I could see that this experience was like the lifting of a heavy weight he had carried around for too long. He told us he had been sent to the southwest, to an area within Ta Mok's zone of operations. In fact, when Ta Mok learned that my brother had run a Chinese restaurant, he made him his personal chef. My brother hated serving this man known as "the butcher" for the brutal executions and purges carried out under his command.

Two children trained as spies had seen him saving scraps of food for the starving people in the camp. After reporting this to their superior, Ta Mok's men seized my brother and ordered him to dig a hole deep enough for him to sit in. He was forced to step into the hole while the dirt was shoveled back on top of him, leaving only his head above the soil level. He was constrained in that hole in the searing heat, while huge ants and other insects bit him and crawled into his eyes, ears, nose, and mouth.

When, at the end of two days, he was removed from the hole, his entire body was covered with bites and terrible sores. He told me that his greatest fear was of being eaten by wild boars or other large animals in the area. He said he was allowed to live only because Ta Mok did not want to lose his cook. After this terrible experience, my brother was filled with anger toward those who had caused so much suffering. He longed for the day when perhaps he could exact revenge upon them.

When my brother's health improved, he and I decided it was safe to return to the cemetery to find our parents' remains. We searched the small Chinese community for an official Scraper and Gatherer of Bones to conduct the rituals for proper exhumation and cleaning of bones with special brushes and cloths before sealing the bones in boxes for onward shipment to China.

The person we found reacted in a strange way when we told him that our parents had been buried in the Choeung Ek cemetery. We did not know that during the Pol Pot era, the orchard was destroyed and large pits dug at Choeung Ek, which became the killing field for the estimated 16,000 people tortured at the infamous Tuol Sleng prison. After being interrogated and tortured at Tuol Sleng, men, women, and children were herded onto trucks and taken to Choeung Ek to be killed and thrown into the pits.

Despite hearing this gruesome news, we insisted on going to the cemetery to pray and make offerings to the spirits of our parents. When we arrived through the south-facing gate, we could see the large empty field and the newly constructed shrine where thousands of skulls are displayed as a reminder of what happened in that killing field. Further in the distance, in the northeastern corner of the field, we saw the gnarled tree and large boulder still standing as silent witnesses to the place where our parents had been buried. Filled with anticipation, we realized that perhaps that part of the cemetery might not have been touched by the bulldozers that had torn up the rest of the cemetery. We cried with joy and held on to each other as we rushed toward the untouched burial place, where we fell to our knees and made offerings to the spirits of our parents.

We arranged for gravediggers to come the next day to remove the caskets so that the bone-gatherer could begin his work. We knew that the coffins had not been buried too deeply in the ground, in the hope that the bodies would decay faster and thus return more quickly to "the lands of Jing and Chu." I feel much more at peace now that I know my parents' bodily remains, as well as their spirits, have returned to the home of their ancestors.

Although I rejoice at having been able to return my parents' remains to their birthplace in China, I know that many Cambodian families have experienced the pain of never knowing where their loved ones were buried. Many of these people come to me to help them deal with their anxiety. They believe that unless a dead one is cremated and buried according to Buddhist traditions, the soul of the deceased will wander throughout the world, weeping and wailing, and perhaps returning to disturb the surviving relatives.

Buddhist monks try to console people by telling them that when a person dies, rebirth will take place according to that person's *karma* (good or bad actions during their lifetime). As long as a person desires existence in the next life, he or she will experience rebirth. Those consoling thoughts, however, do not erase the anxiety of survivors weeping for their loved ones, still unconvinced that their spirits will ever find peace.

****

My main purpose in writing about my experiences is to share my privileged insights into the relationship between Saloth Sar/Pol Pot and Khieu Ponnary. As he became increasingly maniacal, and perhaps even more paranoid than Khieu Ponnary, Pol Pot began to mistrust even those closest to him. He denounced Ieng Sary as a traitor and blamed his deputy Nuon Chea, his main military commander Ta Mok, and Defense Minister Son Sen for military losses as Vietnamese troops began their campaign to oust Pol Pot from power. The last Khmer Rouge figure remaining at Pol Pot's side was Khieu Samphan.

I was especially distressed to learn of the murders of Son Sen and his wife Yun Yat, with whom I had once travelled to Ratanakiri. When they came under suspicion, Pol Pot discovered that they were hiding in an old building not far from his camp near the Thai border. Around midnight, he summoned one of his few remaining military commanders and, in his calm, almost smiling manner, uttered the words he normally used for ordering the liquidation of his enemies: "I would like you to take care of it."

A few hours later, the commander and several of his men located Son Sen and his family. Using rifles, they shot to death not only Son Sen and Yun Yat, but also about ten other family members, including a five-year old grandchild. One former comrade who was close to Son Sen told me that after shooting the family, Pol Pot's men placed the bodies out on the road and drove their trucks several times back and forth over their victims.

Khieu Samphan reportedly approved of these murders, although Nuon Chea and Ta Mok decided that if Pol Pot could kill Son Sen, they would probably be his next victims. Nuon Chea and Ta Mok chased down Pol Pot and placed him under arrest. Soon after, Khieu Samphan also deserted Pol Pot and rallied to Ta Mok's side.

One of my patients, a disaffected Khmer Rouge district chief, told me that Pol Pot's goal of brainwashing people was to create productive, non-feeling, non-thinking beings—more like animals than humans. He told me that he once described life under that regime as a society in which "we grow ignorance.... No schools, no books, no newspapers.... There are no more traditions, no festivals.... My homeland is finished.... The Cambodian no longer exists. Another animal, yes animal, which I cannot recognize, has taken his place."

****

Chapter 4

Patricide
by Marcel Blanchette

I was one of the last foreigners to leave Cambodia after the Khmer Rouge marched into Phnom Penh on 17 April 1975. As they moved through the streets wielding rifles and guns, fierce young people dressed in black gradually took over intersections and commandeered military and civilian vehicles, shouting at residents to leave Phnom Penh because the Americans were going to bomb the capital. These same expressionless and threatening young people ordered all foreigners to move to the French Embassy. As I walked toward the Embassy from my apartment, I saw among the evacuees many sick, wounded, and elderly people moving toward what would become their death march.

This was the beginning of a nightmarish experiment to form a new kind of society populated by those untouched by consumerism or western thought and, therefore, totally loyal to the new all-seeing and all-powerful organization known as Angkar. The rationale for this experiment came from a small group of Khmer communists who had spent the previous few years in isolation in the jungles and remote mountain regions of Cambodia. Their philosophy was so ideologically stern and abstract that it had no regard for the humanity of their victims.

Death of the weak or of anyone who strayed from the precepts of Angkar was condoned as necessary for the success of their revolution.

As I look back at the harm caused to the Khmer soul and culture by those fanatical ideologues, I recall words spoken by Prince Norodom Sihanouk when he returned to his homeland: "My people...had been transformed into cattle [and] my eyes were opened to a madness which neither I nor anyone else had imagined."

As I made my way to seek refuge in the French Embassy, I could not have foreseen the dehumanization, torture, and mass killings that would soon befall the Cambodian people. In fact, many in Phnom Penh initially believed that 17 April 1975 marked the beginning of a new era that would put an end to the corruption and ineptitude that characterized the government of Lon Nol, who had been taken out of the country by his American protectors.

I reached the French Embassy after pushing my way through the throngs of people silently marching in front of their black-clad captors, who periodically fired shots into the air to make them move faster. I wondered what fate awaited all of us who were rushing into the Embassy grounds. One week prior to the takeover, the French government had recognized the Khmer Rouge government; local French diplomats thus assumed they would receive special treatment from the new regime.

At first, the French Embassy opened its doors to anyone seeking asylum, but soon it had to acquiesce to Khmer Rouge demands that it return all Cambodians, Chinese, and Vietnamese seeking asylum there. As we watched a column of about eight hundred walking slowly toward the unknown, those of us who remained were dumbstruck with pity and horror. After the unsuccessful asylum seekers were forced to leave, there remained about one thousand foreigners; of these, seven hundred were French.

Among those Cambodians whom the Khmer Rouge identified as traitors and demanded their surrender was the aristocratic Prince Sisowath Sirik Matak, who walked out calmly before being pushed into a car and driven to his death. Just the week before, he had refused an invitation by the

American Ambassador to be taken in safety to the United States. In a letter to the U.S. Ambassador, Sirik Matak replied, "Dear Excellency and Friend, I cannot...leave in such a cowardly fashion....I have committed [the] mistake of believing in you, the Americans."

Soon after all other Cambodians had vacated the French Embassy grounds, a frail elderly man came seeking asylum. As the duty officer turned him away and into the hands of the Khmer Rouge, the Vice Consul recognized the old man as Prince Norodom Monireth, whom the French had set aside in 1941 in order to place his more malleable nephew, Norodom Sihanouk, on the throne. After having been forced to turn away so many people, the French Vice Consul leaned against one of the pillars at the entrance to the embassy. With tears streaming down his face, he uttered words that could have been spoken by any of Pol Pot's victims: "We are no longer men."

During my stay in the French Embassy, I witnessed many scenes of anxiety and anger as people fought over access to drinking water, toilets, and bathing facilities, as well as to food rationed out by the French diplomats, who often kept the best for themselves. To calm myself during this stressful time, I would often recall my first years in the once peaceful land of gentle people.

****

After majoring in history and specializing in East Asian studies during my years at Laval University in Quebec, I mapped out a plan that would prepare me to travel to Cambodia and to Angkor. Once I completed my university studies in 1963, and with my parents' assistance and the encouragement of my professors at Laval, I went to Paris where I began a comprehensive two-year plan of graduate studies. This included courses at the Sorbonne (Asian history and religions), the National Institute of Oriental Languages and Civilizations (Khmer language and literature), and the National Center of Scientific Research (archeology). I knew that archeological research at the latter facility was affiliated with projects being carried out under the aegis of the French School for Far Eastern Studies/EFEO, which was based in Vietnam but also had branches in Siem Reap and Phnom Penh in Cambodia.

By the time I arrived in Cambodia in 1965, I was proficient in the Khmer language and knowledgeable in Buddhism, Khmer literature, ethnology, and above all, archeology. Once in Phnom Penh, I was assigned by the EFEO office to work on a team led by the brilliant and charismatic Bernard-Philippe Groslier, who introduced modern techniques of field archeology to Cambodia in the 1950s. He was the son of Georges Groslier, the architect, art historian, and a founder of both the Cambodian School for the Arts and the National Museum. Although the younger Groslier never spoke of this himself, I learned from his colleagues that he had been decorated by the French government for heroic service in the Resistance during World War II.

Groslier had an affable, congenial, and extroverted character, unlike most of the French students I had encountered, who seemed guarded and undemonstrative. When I told Bernard-Philippe that he acted more like a Canadian than like most Frenchman I had met during my studies in Paris, he laughed heartily and seemed to enjoy the comparison.

When the dry season afforded easier access to the northwest, I joined Groslier and his team of researchers, architects, and archeologists en route to the EFEO office in Siem Reap. As I rode in a small convoy with supplies and team members, I could see in the distance the magnificent temple of Angkor Wat, with its characteristic five domed towers. This temple complex was completed at the same time as another great twelfth century masterpiece, the Cathedral of Notre Dame in Paris. Like Notre Dame, Angkor represented the central point around which a great civilization would arise. Just as the stained glass pictures and carvings of Notre Dame reveal much about life in France during its earliest days, the carvings and bas-reliefs of Angkor teach us about life in the ancient kingdom of the Khmers.

Although Groslier explained that I would be working with him at the temple of Baphoun, which was built a century before Angkor Wat, he wanted me to become completely familiar with the restoration efforts already begun at Angkor Wat and Angkor Thom. To that end, he assigned a man named Pich Keo, who later became director of the National Museum of Phnom Penh, to serve as my guide for three days. I enjoyed the company of my friend Keo, who loved to talk about the symbolism of Angkor Wat.

"As you no doubt learned in Paris, Marcel, the main body of the temple of Angkor Wat represents the mystical Mount Meru, the center of the universe for believing Hindus. The five peaks of Mount Meru are mirrored in the five symmetrically placed towers of Angkor Wat. The facades of the temple also align with the cardinal points of the compass, with four of the towers set in the four directions (east, west, north, and south) of the larger central tower. The entire structure viewed from above resembles a Mandala, the graphic representation of the multi-layered nature of existence."

"I could observe during my ride here that many of the temples close to the vast Angkor complex are being swallowed up by trees whose roots seem to be spreading out like huge claws or tentacles strangling these structures with all the strength that the tropical rains and heat give to those monsters."

"You observed correctly, Marcel. There are many areas of the Angkor complex that we cannot touch. If we try to remove these huge roots, there is a high risk of destroying the statues and walls they have invaded."

One afternoon Pich Keo and I rested on one of the terraces at Angkor, which seemed completely deserted in the oppressive heat. Nearby we saw a young monk in his orange robe sitting on one of the large stones, chanting his afternoon prayers. Later, a group of children ran in front of us, playing hide-and-seek among the stones. As we made our way to view the bas-reliefs at Angkor Thom, we passed a young girl tending her family's five water buffalo. She seemed too graceful and delicate to be taking care of such large, ugly animals. After our brief stop, we toured some of the fascinating bas-reliefs of Angkor Wat and Angkor Thom.

These carvings depict the lives of all social and political strata of the early Khmer civilization: gods and kings, nobles and priests, warriors and farmers, and peasants and village people. At the bottom is the slave caste, comprised of people who had fallen into debt, criminals, prisoners of war, and members of non-Khmer ethnic groups. Women seem to have played influential roles at all levels of society.

The depictions of gods and kings involve never-ending scenes of combat and ruthless demonstrations of the power of the strong over the weak. They constantly fight over access to the Sea of Milk, which becomes churned up as in a great storm. The elixir produced by this mythical ocean was believed to confer immortality on those who drink from it.

Other bas-reliefs depict scenes of court and religious life, including parades of warriors and musical events where kings, gods, and the graceful female *apsaras* dance to tunes played by instruments similar to western harps, oboes, and lutes, as well as cymbals, gongs, and drums.

The scenes of the daily life of peasants and workers are especially rich in detail. For example, one bas-relief depicts a fisherman standing in his pirogue and fanning out his net onto the waters of the Tonle Sap Lake, while swarms of fish leap out of the water and into his net. One scene depicts a cockfight in progress; in another, a group of men prepares soup by plunging a pig into a huge pot while one man blows into the embers to keep the fire going under the pot. Yet another depicts stone carvers using a variety of tools on the facade of a temple. Beyond that, another wall portrays a young woman about to give birth, holding onto her ankles and crying out as the midwife pushes on her stomach. At the end of this amazing day, we walked along the Terrace of the Elephants, where replicas of these huge animals and their riders are carved into the terrace wall.

That night I had dreams that gave life to the kaleidoscopic images I had witnessed during the day, reflecting the immortal beauty of Angkor and its culture. In my dream, I could almost feel the thunderous rumbling of the ground as a herd of female elephants passed before me and stopped while they raised their trunks to herald the arrival of their leader. On top of the large bull elephant sat Jayavarman VII on an ornate gold and red throne. Courtiers dressed in colorful silks surrounded the king and created shade for him with their long-handled red silk umbrellas with gold tassels.

Next, I dreamt that the lovely girl I saw tending her family's water buffalo rose up and changed into one of the graceful celestial dancers known as *apsaras* whose backward-bent fingers and rich headdress and costumes portrayed on the walls of Angkor are reflected today in the dancers of the Royal Cambodian Ballet. As the delicate *apsara* glided across the terrace, a cloud of orange butterflies swooped down and carried her upward with them, until she soon disappeared from view. As the setting sun gave a golden hue to the towers of the main temple and gradually descended toward the horizon, I saw and heard in my dream a line of orange-robed monks chanting and moving slowly toward their monastery outside the temple grounds.

****

As I approached the site of the temple at Baphuon (Ba Puon in Khmer), I could not believe the enormity of the task ahead. I had seen watercolor reproductions of the temple while in Paris and could not believe what time and the elements had done to the temple, which now seemed collapsed onto itself from within. As I moved closer, I discovered Groslier standing amid what appeared to be a huge jigsaw puzzle of stones placed around the perimeter of the original structure and among the trees in the surrounding forests.

During the next few days, I learned more about what caused the disintegration of this enormous structure described by a 13th century Chinese diplomat as a "mountain of bronze...a truly astonishing spectacle...." [These words can also translate to "mountain of gold."] Unfortunately, its sheer size, and the manner in which the huge towers and other elements were held together, carried the seeds of its own destruction from the beginning of its construction.

Groslier pointed out that the Baphuon temple originally measured 130 meters wide by 104 meters long and over 50 meters high. The central core of the pyramidal-shaped temple was an artificial hill of sand on which a large Hindu shrine previously stood. Three large stone galleries, each superimposed on the other, were also filled with sand. Sadly, the stone retaining walls built around each of the three levels were too thin to be effective. Over the centuries, water from monsoon rains gradually seeped through the sandstone walls, adding to the weight of the sand within, thus causing entire sections to collapse. Some of the worst damage was caused by a particularly devastating monsoon in 1943.

Avoiding mistakes made over the years by others who tried to restore the temple, Groslier decided to use a technique known as anastylosis. An EFEO architect learned this technique in Greece, where it has been used since 1902 to restore Greek temples and a collapsed portion of the Parthenon. Anastylosis involves removing components and later repositioning them in their original space, which is obviously much easier in theory than in practice.

In order to apply this technique to the immense temple at Baphuon, each of the 300,000 stones on the exterior had to be dismantled one by one and meticulously numbered, with the location of each removed stone recorded in Groslier's notebook. He explained to me that there was no room for error because, as in a jigsaw, each block of stone had its own dimensions, and none were interchangeable.

By the time that I arrived in Siem Reap, Groslier's team had already shored up the sandfill with cement, stabilized the first of the three levels, and removed most of the 300,000 stones. This work was backbreaking and had taken several years, but the workers were treated well and took pride in restoring an important element of Cambodia's heritage. Groslier and his team of French experts gladly shared their knowledge with their Cambodian counterparts. At the end of each day, they celebrated together their large and small accomplishments and discussed how things might be improved or changed to help them reach near- and long-term goals. From observing Groslier and his colleagues, I learned much about real leadership, as well as about archeology.

****

Before travel beyond our site at Baphuon became increasingly dangerous, I was able to make small forays into surrounding villages. One of my favorite small trips was to the village of Puok, about sixteen kilometers west of Siem Reap, where Cham families have produced beautiful silks for clothing and fabrics for draperies and other decorative purposes since the days of the Silk Road. The Muslim Chams cultivated mulberry trees and carefully nurtured special silkworms that produced a silky substance, which was transformed into thread colored with dyes from plants and berries of the region and woven by the women into intricate patterns.

Whenever we needed new sandstone, a small group of us would go by truck to the highlands about twenty kilometers to the northeast of Angkor, specifically to Phnom Kulen. This elevated area was the source of all the water that filled the canals and reservoirs of Angkor, as well as for the sandstone used by the sculptors and stonemasons.

During each excursion beyond the temples and monuments, I was amazed at the variety of life around us, especially the tall *dipterocarp* trees that reach heights from fifty to seventy-five meters, and from whose broad-leafed branches hang pendulous red and pink wing-like pods. Within these pods grows a type of nut that people in the area sold in the local markets. People also looked to these trees as a source of aromatic oils and resin. While walking through the forests of Siem Reap, I noticed many of the smooth trunks scarred by blackened cavities where people had dug into them to extract the resin.

Within the forests, I enjoyed watching the gibbons and macaques moving among the trees. Sometimes I would see groups of kingfisher birds, their iridescent blue feathers contrasting with the coral-red of their bills, breasts, and necks. One night after I recounted to my colleagues how struck I was by the beauty of these small birds, Pick Keo expounded, "I have always enjoyed watching these little birds that eat small fish from streams and the Tonle Sap Lake. They find high perches along the water's edge, from which they can search for schools of small fish. They then plunge straight down and emerge soon after, holding their prey in their long, pointy beaks. At other times, they hover over the water, bills pointed downward, before diving into the water for fish. I have heard that they have special membranes that protect their eyes when they are in the water. Once they return to their perches, they beat the fish against branches to dislodge the fish bones. They are truly amazing little hunters!"

Groslier shared, "I have just been reading the diary of a twelfth century Chinese envoy to Cambodia who said that Chinese visitors to the kings of Angkor always left with bags of blue kingfisher feathers, which they used for ornamentation on courtiers' headdresses."

Our conversation then turned to a variety of topics, including Khmer rituals and culture. "While working in this idyllic area so closely linked to the origins of Khmer culture," I told Groslier, "I often experience a profound sense of the sacred in listening to the soft chanting of monks in nearby monasteries or witnessing the rituals of people making offerings to the *neak ta*."

"Yes, Marcel, I believe we all experience those same feelings working in what is essentially a sacred place. Despite the influence of Hinduism and Buddhism, Cambodians have never lost their belief in these spirits that ensure the well-being of inhabitants of each village. Local villagers believe that Angkor Wat houses several of these spirits, the most important of which is Ta Reach, who local people say is depicted in bodily form in the Vishnu statue on the west gallery of Angkor Wat. On specific days each year, villagers make offerings to Ta Reach and other spirits that protect Angkor Wat. These ceremonies are usually accompanied by music or dance to appease the spirits. Tomorrow, before we begin the work on the next section at Baphuon, you will witness one of these ceremonies."

That day, the Khmer craftsmen and technicians on our team inaugurated the undertaking in the same way that Khmer artists and artisans have done for centuries; namely, with a ceremony honoring Pisnokar (the Hindu, Bisnukara), the legendary divine architect of Angkor Wat. Before building a house or an ox cart, designing a silver bracelet, or making a new article of clothing, Cambodians make offerings to Pisnokar, who they believe will bring success to the work and blessings upon its creators. Even today, long after the attempts by Pol Pot to destroy all aspects of Khmer tradition and culture, people continue to make offerings to their specific *neak ta*, as well as to Buddha and the Hindu divinities.

The ceremony honoring our new project began early in the evening after we walked reverently up the 200-meter elevated sandstone walkway, worn smooth by the thousands who walked before us over the centuries. Once at the terrace of Baphuon, we enjoyed a delicious meal of sweet rice dumplings, grilled chicken with papaya, fish caught that day in the Tonle Sap Lake, and fresh fruits. As the sun began to set, our Khmer colleagues placed offerings on a table facing the temple: small plates of food, one bowl of rice, one candle, four coins, one piece of cloth, and one piece of paper money.

A thin blind man holding a stringed instrument was led to a bench in front of the table, where he sat facing the spectators. He was one of the wandering poets who travel throughout the countryside recounting tales from Hindu mythology, or merely telling folk tales or local news events. He raised his instrument, known as a *chapay*, a two-stringed, long-necked lute whose bottom string is for rhythm and top string for melody. His voice and his instrument alternated, conveying the message itself and the underlying feelings best expressed by instrument alone. He stood still, his face raised to the sky whose red-orange rays lent a beatific aura to his countenance. He sang with a controlled passion, in sonorous tones emanating from deep within his throat and chest, making me shudder in the presence of such an unearthly sound. While I could not understand all the words of the song, its overall message was one of melancholy and loss.

When the blind poet finished, the table with the offerings was moved to the side while a large white screen held up by two tall bamboo posts was placed in front of us; we were about to be entertained by a traditional Khmer shadow theater group. During the days of the Angkorian kings, these shadow puppet shows had a sacred aspect and were performed only on specific occasions such as the New Year or the king's birthday. Later, even though they became accessible to the larger public, they retained a mystical dimension. Each figure is made of a single piece of leather, usually two meters in height and decorated with intricate openwork. Once the artisan has drawn the desired character or figure on the tanned hide, he cuts it and treats it with a dye from the bark of the Kandaol tree. He then paints it and attaches two long bamboo sticks with which to control the puppet.

Before the show began, large torches were lit behind the screen, where the puppet masters waited until the fire gave sufficient illumination to project the silhouettes of the puppets onto the screen. While the shadow figures enacted scenes from the *Ramayana* (the Khmer version is called *Ream-ker*), a group of musicians played a variety of traditional Khmer instruments, including gongs, oboes, and drums, as well as the *roneat,* a type of xylophone. I once read that the young Saloth Sar loved to play this instrument as a secondary school student.

The final presentation was by a line of men playing long drums known as *chhayam,* accompanied by male and female dancers making percussive sounds with cymbals or hand-held wooden clackers. The drummers led several rounds of call-and-response singing, which soon involved all the Khmer workers surrounding the stage, as well as villagers who had stopped by to enjoy the evening's presentations.

During my brief two-year stay in Siem Reap, I sometimes heard this call-and-response singing wafting up from the rice paddies as men and women chanted back and forth to ease the burden of their work. This type of vocalizing reminded me very much of the soulful music associated with African-American slaves and the blues singers inspired by them.

On the following day, I commented to Groslier that I was struck by the overall sadness and often violent tone of the artistic presentations we had witnessed the night before. He then made a startling observation about the Khmer people that I have never forgotten. He said that beneath the famous Khmer smile reside dark, foreboding forces. His exact words that I recorded in my journal were "Beneath a carefree surface there slumber savage forces and disconcerting cruelties which may blaze up at any time in outbreaks of passionate brutality."

****

By early 1970, events moved so quickly that I find it hard to place them in order. While we were still in Siem Reap, we heard news of the coup against Sihanouk by Lon Nol, a man many considered weak and inept. Then came the astonishing news that Sihanouk was in Beijing and had joined forces with the Khmer Rouge.

Increasing numbers of refugees came to our worksite seeking protection from the growing conflict around us, and from Khmer Rouge leaders forcing villagers to relocate and live under their draconian rules of discipline and indoctrination. We could see and hear increasing evidence of North Vietnamese and Khmer Rouge inroads into the entire Angkor area. The peaceful sounds of gongs, temple bells, and chanting monks were drowned out by mortar fire, and the Vietnamese set up 105mm howitzer positions just north of the Grand Hotel in Siem Reap.

Even though we were many miles away from areas to our east where American B-52 planes were dropping tons of bombs against alleged Vietnamese sanctuaries, we could feel the vibrations and hear the distant roar of the planes. Word spread quickly throughout the country of the devastation this bombing campaign was having on the people and the countryside now defaced by huge craters.

Around April, we had to abandon our office, which forced us to pack and remove precious documents and artifacts and transport them by truck and small aircraft to Phnom Penh. Once in the capital city, Groslier moved into the lovely ochre and cream villa where four generations of his family had lived since the early days of the French protectorate. This beautiful home was filled with priceless temple rubbings, carvings, pottery, and other types of early Khmer art. Unlike most foreign diplomats and wealthy Cambodians, Groslier refused to have armed guards posted in front of his home, even as thousands of refugees poured into the city and crime increased.

I moved into one of the small bungalows belonging to the Phnom Hotel, which was close to Groslier's home and to the new EFEO offices. The other bungalows, lined up next to the hotel's outdoor restaurant and pool, were being used by international aid workers sent to Cambodia to deal with the huge influx of refugees into the capital city. Until the Khmer Rouge takeover, I felt that my EFEO colleagues and the idealistic aid workers I met in Phnom Penh, like the Buddhist monks throughout the country, were playing equally important roles in the protection and restoration of Cambodia's precious heritage.

In 1972, almost two years after our team had brought truckloads of documents and artifacts from Siem Reap to Phnom Penh, we finally managed to complete the time-consuming tasks of cataloging them and locating appropriate storage spaces either in our new office or at the National Museum. To thank the Khmer and French members of this unique team of archeologists, engineers, historians, and restoration specialists, Groslier organized a dinner at his beautiful villa.

Because the dinner took place during the height of the rainy season, the garden area leading to the villa was completely inundated with several inches of rain that had fallen during the early evening and would not likely be absorbed into the ground for a few more hours. To deal with this situation, Groslier set up a walkway of boards built upon stones that would allow us to make our way to the entrance without getting our feet wet. As I walked along this pathway of wood, the sky became black even though it was not yet night, and the deafening roar of thunder drowned out the sounds of the mortar and rocket fire to which we had become accustomed during the past few years.

As I approached the main entrance, a golden light radiated from inside the house, spilling out over the steps leading to the home. Once I reached the top step, I could see dozens of candelabra and mirrored plates filled with candles throughout the front rooms, lending these spaces a soft golden hue. Inside the house, the scent of the candles mixed with the perfume of bouquets of jasmine, lilies, and other fragrant flowers that graced the dining table, serving tables, and other large surfaces. As we arrived, Groslier explained:

After a bolt of lightning struck a nearby power station, we lost all power in this area and have been told that it will not likely be repaired for several hours.

Because we know that these severe rains will continue for the next few days, there is not much likelihood that the power will return any time soon.

So, my friends, we had to innovate! I asked my cook and housekeeper to set out all the candles you can see inside, while I installed an outdoor charcoal-fueled stove on the covered veranda at the rear of the house. And voila! Everything is ready, and no possible electricity outage will interfere with our dinner!

Next to the dining room, we could hear the gentle sounds of traditional Khmer music. Groslier explained that to set the tone for an evening of good conversation and camaraderie, he had invited a trio of musicians (one playing the *roneat* and two playing the lute-like stringed instruments we had heard at ceremonies in Siem Reap). Later, as we enjoyed a delicious dinner of French and Cambodian specialties accompanied by French wines, the murmuring sounds of the Khmer music made the perfect background to our conversation and enjoyment of the cuisine. There was more than enough food for everyone even though many guests came with their spouses.

After dinner, the women—except for the female members of the EFEO team—moved to a separate room for dessert, card games, and liqueur. Our team members lingered until late into the evening, sipping brandy and discussing the work we had already accomplished and what type of work remained to be done prior to our return to Siem Reap, which we hoped would not be too far into the future.

One of the French archeologists asked Groslier if he thought it would be best to ship all that we had brought from Siem Reap back to the EFEO offices in Paris for safekeeping, especially in light of the precarious situation in Phnom Penh. Groslier disagreed vehemently, "I believe strongly that the precious scholarly research and material we so diligently preserved during our time in Siem Reap should be retained in Phnom Penh to demonstrate our commitment to future generations of Cambodians. We will not send it back to Paris!"

When we left the villa at about 11:00 pm, I looked around one more time at the beautiful white tile floor with its delicate green and gold leaf designs. The highly polished rosewood furniture was upholstered in a silk fabric mirroring the colors and designs of the tile floors. Every smaller table held a single precious object framed by orchids appropriate to the size and form of the artifact on display. On the buttery yellow walls, impressive temple rubbings from Angkor Wat depicted scenes of the violent stories of the *Ramayana* where the battles between god-kings and demons continually churn up the Sea of Milk to gain access to its liquor of immortality.

I fell asleep soon after I reached my bungalow behind the Phnom Hotel. After what seemed to be a very short period (probably an hour or two), I was awakened by someone pounding on my door. I ran to see who it was and recognized the son of Groslier's housekeeper, the marvelous woman responsible for the decorations and flower arrangements I had admired that evening. The boy, around fourteen years old, just kept shouting, "Something very bad has happened! Come quickly!" As I approached the front gate to the villa, I met two of my associates who had also been awakened by members of Groslier's household staff. I noticed that the electricity had now been restored. In contrast to the soft golden candle light I had seen earlier, the light from the front entrance now seemed too bright and too cold.

I could not believe what I saw as I entered the front room. All the furniture had been overturned or broken; precious objects were missing or smashed; and ugly streaks of red spattered the white tiled floor, gold and white draperies, and lovely furniture coverings. There were splashes of this red substance on the walls and temple rubbings as well.

Suddenly we all understood what had happened; the red substance spilled all over the room was the blood of our beloved colleague. His body, lying between the main room and the dining area, was covered with horrible knife wounds. So much blood had emptied onto the floor that we could not believe he was still alive. The cook and the housekeeper told us that they had hidden in the kitchen after hearing one or perhaps two men break into the house, apparently to steal whatever they could find. Groslier, a strong, sturdily built man, evidently had surprised his attackers and put up a super-human fight to protect the home of his ancestors and the precious objects each generation had accumulated. All the noise generated by the fight must have startled the would-be burglars, who had escaped as lights suddenly came on in the residence. At that point, the two women had looked in and seen Groslier's bloodied body on the floor. Afraid to move him, they had dispatched their children to round up any of his colleagues living nearby.

One colleague ran to wake up Doctor Lepelletier, the chief surgeon at Calmette Hospital, while I went in search of a *cyclo* in which another colleague and I would try to carry Groslier to Calmette. Along the way, I met a group of soldiers with two jeeps, guarding one of the many checkpoints set up throughout the city after the official curfew hours. I explained the seriousness of the situation to the soldiers, who rushed back with me in one of the jeeps to bring Groslier to the hospital. I was relieved to find these men because I doubted Groslier would survive the bumpy, slow-moving *cyclo* ride from east of the Wat Phnom, west toward the Phnom Hotel and French Cathedral, and then north toward the hospital.

My colleague who had remained behind with Groslier was able to use towels and sheets provided by the housekeeper to stop some of the bleeding. The soldiers proved to be especially valuable since they were able to make splints to deal right away with serious wounds to the arms and legs. There were also terrible wounds to the neck, chest, and abdomen that only a surgeon could address. The soldiers fashioned a type of stretcher made of rugs and wooden poles, which they laid across the back of the jeep as the two of us held onto our unconscious friend and colleague. Thanks to this mode of transportation, we brought Groslier to Calmette Hospital a good hour before our third companion arrived with Dr. Lepelletier, who was initially reluctant and had to be convinced that this was truly an emergency.

After the first surgical operation to save Groslier's life, Doctor Lepelletier concluded that his patient's chances of recovery would be better in Phnom Penh than if he were moved abroad. For another year, Groslier remained in Phnom Penh while undergoing more surgeries, transfusions, and therapies aimed at restoring him to some level of normalcy. Groslier's strength of spirit and determination surprised the doctors and nurses at Calmette, who marveled at his ability to keep working and meeting with the EFEO team while recuperating.

At the end of a year's treatment at Calmette, however, Groslier followed his doctors' advice and moved to Bangkok, where there were larger medical facilities designed to deal with the types of wounds he had suffered. When our EFEO team accompanied Groslier to Pochentong Airport in Phnom Penh, many of us held back tears as this brave and charismatic leader flew to Thailand. Before his departure, he insisted that he would return as soon as the military situation in Cambodia was resolved sufficiently to resume work on the restoration of the temple of Baphuon.

I saw Groslier years later during a visit to the EFEO office in Paris. At that time, he expressed the hope that he could one day return to Cambodia to complete the restoration. Sadly, he died in 1986 at age sixty, disappointed at never being able to return to Baphuon or to look once again at the work he had done at Angkor Wat and Angkor Thom.

After traveling to Paris to attend Groslier's funeral, I returned to Quebec City to resume teaching at the University of Laval. During regular phone conversations with my former EFEO colleagues, we often discussed our hope of eventually returning to Cambodia to complete the project most dear to Groslier—the restoration of the Baphoun temple.

****

When in June 1995 my team of French archeologists, engineers, and scholars decided to resume and complete our long-delayed restoration of the Baphuon temple, we faced an almost impossible task. First, we had to survey the damage done since the closing of the Siem Reap office in 1970 and assess how best to tackle this daunting project that had been so dear to our former colleague, Bernard-Philippe Groslier.

We could not leave Phnom Penh immediately because Cambodia was at the height of its rainy season. While this would normally be just a minor setback, this year it brought disastrous floods to the northwestern parts of the country, as it had done in 1993. These floods cut off the main supply lines between the rice- and fish-producing areas along the Tonle Sap Lake, causing serious food shortages in the central and southern provinces. Each day the local news brought terrible stories of farmers, children, animals, and homes swept away in the floods. The rampaging waters also destroyed large areas of rice fields and farmland. We were eager to leave for Siem Reap but had to wait until the dry season began in the fall.

When our EFEO team, led by architect Pascal Royère who had previously worked in Siem Reap with Bernard-Philippe Groslier, finally arrived at the site of the Baphuon temple, we were overwhelmed at what we saw. At the time of Groslier's first visit in the 1960s, he had seen only a huge crumbling mass of stone lying on top of a collapsed sandfill. When we returned in 1995, our first impression of the once-revered temple was of a large mountain of red laterite, the material Groslier had used to encase the temple after he had shored up the sandfill with cement.

When we looked around for the stones removed prior to our departure from Siem Reap in 1970, we discovered all 300,000 stones lying about, spread over 10 hectares (about 24.7 acres). Many of the stones were at least partially engulfed in jungle vegetation. As a result, the numbers on some stones had completely disappeared. Without Groslier's notes showing where each numbered stone fit, the remaining numbers meant nothing. We would have to find some other way to determine where each stone fit into the overall design of the temple. As with any puzzle, only one piece could fit in any given spot. If one stone were wrongly placed, it would be impossible to restore the surface of the temple. We soon realized the magnitude of the task before us and calculated that it would take us almost two years to figure out exactly how the stones had originally been organized.

We did finally succeed in our effort, thanks to three important factors. Retired EFEO architect Jacques Dumarcay, who had supervised the Baphuon project for Groslier in the 1960s, was part of our team. Also, to our great joy, about thirty Cambodian technicians and workers from the 1960s project spontaneously arrived just one day after our team reached Siem Reap. Last, but not least, we learned that the EFEO office in Paris had retained photographic records of all the work done at Baphuon.

When our Cambodian technicians and workers arrived, we embraced them with great emotion. We had feared the Khmer Rouge had killed them all. We asked Mith Priem, who became a key supervisor at the site, how they had survived.

"As you can see, we are all alive and intact! All the conservationists and technicians were kept together and given special protection at a cooperative in Siem Reap, in anticipation that our talents and skills would be needed in the construction of monuments to Pol Pot and the Khmer Rouge. During our years of so-called protection under the Khmer Rouge, we often talked about and planned for our eventual return to Baphuon. We know how to recognize patterns on stone and to manage stone research teams. And, just as important, we can train others to do this and to organize the work. We are ready to join you in this important undertaking!"

Together with the scientific memory of Dumarcay and the technical ability of the Khmer workers, we could see that the project would become less daunting and more manageable. Pascal Royère stated, "Without one or the other, this project would have been very difficult."

Although Groslier's written notes had been destroyed, Dumarcay recalled that since the beginning of their work at Angkor, EFEO researchers had taken photos of each monument, retaining one copy in Phnom Penh and sending another to their office in Paris. After hearing this, we immediately sent a telegram to our colleagues in Paris, who discovered 940 photos of the Baphuon temple, dating back to 1910. These pictures showed us exactly what the moldings and sculpted patterns looked like, and which portions of the monument were already missing in 1910, so that we would not have to search for stones that were never there. We completed the restoration of Baphuon in 2011.

****

Today, more than forty years after the end of the Pol Pot regime, it is clear that the concepts of state and responsible governance remain nonexistent. Anything and anybody can be bought or sold. The entire system rests on bribery and competition for power and sources of enrichment. Unemployment levels have reached as high as fifty percent, and over half of the population lives in poverty. People are so desperate to find jobs that they are ready to pay enormous bribes to obtain any kind of work. A recent World Bank study concluded that the level of bribery in Cambodia is twice as significant as in Bangladesh, which has long been considered one of the most corrupt nations in the world.

The principal cause of the current devastating floods and other destruction of Cambodia's natural resources is the large-scale deforestation begun by the Khmer Rouge who cut down large swathes of forest to sell to Thai business interests. As huge areas of Cambodia's forests were denuded, rich topsoil consequentially washed away. From the Tonle Sap Lake to provinces in the south, the beneficial floods that had enriched the land for centuries now instead dump tons of mud onto once-fertile farmland. Although the Cambodian government periodically announced bans on the sale of timber to Thailand, these efforts were meaningless, and the trading of wood continues unabated. The Hun Sen government eventually ceased such sales to Thailand but immediately signed two new deals: a sixty-year logging concession for a Malaysian company to harvest four percent of Cambodia's forestland and a fifty-year concession for an Indonesian firm to harvest another fifteen percent. This does not bode well for the future sustainability of Cambodia's forest reserves, which has seen a loss of over seventy-five percent of its primary rainforest since 1990. A United Nations study identified Cambodia as having one of the highest rates of deforestation in the world.

Harm to Cambodia's agriculture and environment has been further exacerbated by an extensive program of dam building and blasting of rapids further north in China. In addition to reducing the amount of fresh water flowing southward into

Cambodia, these programs make Cambodia increasingly vulnerable to poisoning of the food supply from pesticide and heavy industry runoff in China. Many species of large fish, including the freshwater dolphins of the lower Mekong, are already seriously endangered and may disappear if these programs continue.

Cambodia does not yet have a government freely elected by the people. Former Khmer Rouge commanders, who fill many senior positions within the government and military, actively encourage people to forget the crimes of Pol Pot. This regime adopted a practice that many years ago marked the nadir of Norodom Sihanouk's rule; namely, the opening of casinos throughout the country. In Phnom Penh alone, there are over twenty such establishments, whose main purpose is to launder dirty money. Residents of Phnom Penh who abhor this situation claim that every time a casino is built, Prime Minister Hun Sen pockets two million dollars.

Hun Sen, the ruling party, and the military have also been implicated in other unsavory activities, such as narcotics trafficking. The United Nations Office on Drugs and Crime recently concluded that the "military forces are frequently more a part of the drug trafficking problem than its solution." Traditionally a drug-trafficking route and large marijuana producer, Cambodia has also become a center for the production of crystal methamphetamine, known as "ice." There have been several large arrests at the airport for possession of palladium, an integral ingredient in the processing of this drug; another arrest included the seizure of a machine capable of producing ten thousand ice tablets per hour.

Every day on the streets of Phnom Penh, I see evidence of the large-scale dependence of young people on ice, a highly addictive drug that causes paranoia, delusions, and hallucinations. It is sad to see growing numbers of young people, with crude tattoos and scabs on their upper arms, living on the streets of the city. One local non-governmental organization produced a study showing that while twelve percent of street children in Phnom Penh were using methamphetamine in the year 2000, this practice had risen to almost ninety percent by 2012. Thanks to the work of outraged citizens, pressure has been put on the government to cease arresting and putting these young people in prison, and instead, to place them in rehabilitation centers. This effort sounds promising, but the high rates of unemployment often lead young people back to drug abuse.

In addition to drug trafficking and production, Cambodia has also become a center for the smuggling and exploitation of human beings, kidnappings, prostitution, illegal gambling, arms trafficking, and extortion. Crime syndicates and others involved in these repulsive practices are too often protected by Cambodian officials.

Equally appalling is a mindset that is too prevalent in Cambodia; namely, the "culture of impunity." From the god-kings of Angkor, to Pol Pot, and later, to Hun Sen, no rulers or high-level perpetrators have ever been brought to account. For this reason, crime is rampant and anarchy rules on the streets. One criminal rationalized his actions by claiming, "The Khmer Rouge killed many. They were never punished. Any crimes I might commit would be less than those of the Khmer Rouge. They got away with it. Why should I not do the same?"

I am also appalled at the extent to which many Cambodians, both here and overseas, have demonstrated a desire to forget the past, including the crimes of the Khmer Rouge. I watched a video of Pol Pot's capture in 1997 when he and three local commanders were brought before a mass meeting at the Thai border to be questioned by journalists. Pol Pot, looking like a frail old man, sat in a chair holding a long bamboo cane in one hand and a rattan fan in the other. Rather than questioning the former despot about the crimes he had committed, his captors took a surprisingly deferential tone, speaking in a gentle, almost respectful manner. When the Khmer Rouge leader left the interview, some people bowed, as if to royalty. An American journalist who interviewed Pol Pot shortly before his death found the old man chillingly unrepentant. Pol Pot told the journalist, "My conscience is clear....My life is over politically and personally."

In one of the of the regions still dominated by former Khmer Rouge, residents of Anlong Veng have unveiled a mausoleum copied from the ancient temples of Angkor to honor Ta Mok, widely known as "the butcher" because of the particularly cruel ways in which he tortured and murdered thousands of people. Even Duch, who ran the infamous prison at Tuol Sleng, criticized Ta Mok's tactics in a statement to a western journalist, "I told [people] they would be released if they talked. This was a lie, but it worked. Ta Mok just tortured and killed them."

Ta Mok, who died in prison in 2006, is revered in Anlong Veng, where one resident said, "We regarded Ta Mok like a father who takes care of his children." He built roads, a hospital, and school buildings with wealth he and other former Khmer Rouge amassed from the smuggling and sale of gems and timber into Thailand, as well as the practices of patronage and corruption that have characterized Cambodian governments for generations. The town's three thousand schoolchildren know little or nothing about the crimes perpetrated by Ta Mok and other Khmer Rouge leaders. It appears that the citizens of Anlong Veng, like many other Cambodians, took to heart the words of Hun Sen, who claims "we must dig a hole into which we can bury the past."

****

Despite my dismay at what has happened to the Cambodian people and their land, I still have hope for the future. I recently took a short trip to Takhmau, southwest of Phnom Penh, to visit the Institute for Khmer Traditional Textiles that has revived the art of silk weaving in Cambodia. The weavers who for generations maintained this art were for the most part Muslim Cham women, who either fled with their families or were killed in Pol Pot's purges of the Chams. Today ethnic Khmer, as well as Chams, work together weaving traditional silk designs. Mulberry trees necessary for the cultivation of silk worms have been planted in the area, thus providing one small but significant way in which the fabric of Cambodian identity is being restored.

On my way back from Takhmau, I stopped at a village where people gathered around a small temple, their hands joined and raised upward in prayer while they bowed inward. Placed on an altar inside was an odd-looking statue of the Buddha covered with garlands of flowers and surrounded by sticks of incense placed in large sand-filled bowls. The statue's eyes were missing, as well as an arm, a foot, and one side of its head.

As I listened to the people and monks chanting, one villager explained to me that most of the original population had died under the Khmer Rouge regime. Despite this overwhelming loss, the people were smiling and singing to this shattered statue of the Buddha. He added that when people returned to the village after the war, they discovered pieces of the statue in streams, under trees, and in the fields. Even though they could not piece together the entire statue, the villagers believe that the spirit of the Buddha is there again to console and protect them.

****

When thinking about a meaningful way to describe the magnitude of what happened to Cambodia, I turned to the writings of one of my favorite thinkers, the Roman orator Cicero. He used the word "patriacide," the willful destruction of an entire country—a term that goes beyond "genocide," the destruction of a particular ethnic or religious group. Patriacide more closely describes Pol Pot's compulsion to destroy all aspects of Khmer life and even to erase Cambodia's past. Pol Pot forced his victims to live like unfeeling robots, with no consolation for their present life and no hope for the future. This great crime of the Khmer Rouge has made it extremely difficult for Cambodians to reclaim the past that was stolen from them.

I also find these words of Cicero especially pertinent to the situation in Cambodia: "To be ignorant of what occurred before you were born is to remain always a child." Just as the mulberry trees and silkworms have been delicately restored, the battered Buddha put back into place, and the 300,000 stones of Baphuon replaced one by one, the collective Cambodian memory must be put together again. Only then can the past, present, and future of the country be seen as an unbreakable continuum—just as the Buddha taught. That is why I chose to add my recollections to those of others seeking to reinforce Cambodia's memory of the harm caused by the Khmer Rouge.

Ieng Sary, Ieng Thirith, Nuon Chea, and Khieu Samphan were arrested in 2007 and scheduled to be brought before a joint United Nations–Cambodian tribunal for crimes against humanity. But those trials were repeatedly delayed by interference of the Hun Sen government and inaction on the part of the United Nations. As these frail, elderly mass murderers either died or were found unfit for trial, few believed any possible sentences could equate with the brutality of their crimes, or that any prison accommodations could ever be as severe as those of their victims in the torture centers and killing fields of the Khmer Rouge.

Many young people are skeptical about what their elders say they endured and witnessed under the Khmer Rouge. In the absence of a shared national story, a large number of young Cambodians of the early 21st century represent a "lost generation." Yet we must teach them that the past is not dead but rather lives on in the testimony of those who went before. If the Cambodian people are to know themselves, they must be reconnected to all the beauty and riches, as well as the dark periods, of their past.

Throughout my lifetime, I have admired the valuable contributions to Khmer life and culture made by the exemplary lives of Buddhist monks, as well as Khmer artists, poets, and musicians. They are the ones who will eventually find a way to heal the wounds caused to the Khmer people by unworthy leaders whose attempts to repress memories of the past will eventually fail. Honest leaders and ordinary men and women can create the conditions for proper stewardship of the land and responsible governance of its inhabitants.

It is the responsibility of Cambodia's poets, musicians, artists, and writers to create needed linkages between this beautiful country's past and present. Only they can do this in ways that touch the souls of the Khmer people. I believe the following words of the great Cambodian poet U Sam Oeur represent the best way to express my plea for national enlightenment. This is from a book of poetry given to me by my long-time friend and Buddhist monk, the Venerable Hem Narong.

The ruins of Angkor cry out!
O Poets! Listen to the ruins!
They are wailing, the temple of Bayon cries aloud.
"Have pity on the Khmer people!" They suffer still.
O Cambodian Poets, please cast poems to
       subdue the enemy.
Angkor Wat, our most sublime monument,
       weeps and sobs.
[Poets], liberate our country from tyranny.

****

Acknowledgments

First, I thank Ben Kiernan, Director of Yale University's MacMillan Center for International and Global Studies, who encouraged me to write this book. He led the effort to preserve and copy in digital format the Khmer Rouge archives discovered in the Cambodian Ministry of Interior in 1996. This treasure trove of data was invaluable in my efforts to understand the Khmer Rouge organization and leaders.

Many Western aid workers, especially Larry Bourassa and Reverend Philip McNamara of Catholic Relief Services, shared their insights into living conditions in cities and remote villages where they brought food, clothing, and shelter to those escaping from the Khmer Rouge—and from American bombing raids. Sister Angela Daniels and Reverend Daniel Trainor, who worked with Cambodian refugees in Thailand and helped to resettle those who came to Rhode Island to work in its then-thriving jewelry industry, described for me the dangers faced by Cambodians in Thai refugee camps and the difficulties many experienced in trying to adapt to life in the West.

The late V. James Fazio, a former State Department officer and senior briefer for the White House Situation Room in the 1970s, helped me sift through the correspondence between Prime Minister Lon Nol and President Richard Nixon, and helped to place that material in the proper context.

Youk Chhang, Director of the Documentation Center of Cambodia, provided invaluable assistance with regard to authentic Khmer spellings of words and names. He also shared his personal insights into the damage caused to Cambodia by the brutal Pol Pot regime.

Several individuals provided invaluable editorial assistance. Literary editor Alice Rosengard generously provided expert guidance and suggestions during the preparation of the final draft of the manuscript. I owe a great debt of gratitude to Pat Chaney for her words of encouragement and help throughout the whole process—from writing query letters and synopses to the various stages of the manuscript itself. I especially value her impressive work with regard to style, format, and organizational issues. Brown University professor emeritus and author Henry Majewsky (one of my former professors at Brown graduate school) edited earlier drafts of this book.

Everett Lewis, generous neighbor as well as IT guru and expert webmaster, provided invaluable assistance in setting up the *FourFacesofTruth.com* webpage that, in turn, facilitated the all-important public relations and marketing efforts for the book.

I thank everyone associated with the annual Ocean State Writers' Conference, especially Richard Hoffman, senior writer-in-residence at Emerson College in Boston, and Jody Lisberger, instructor in Creative Writing and head of Women's Studies at the University of Rhode Island.

Jean Israel of the U.S. National Archives helped to collate the correspondence between Prime Minister Lon Nol and U.S. President Richard Nixon, which was not stored in the Nixon Library but rather in a classified section at the National Archives. The support of Markus Wiener, publisher of my nonfiction book *Born at the Battlefield of Gettysburg; an African-American Family Saga* (Markus Wiener Publishers, Princeton NJ) gave me the confidence to take on this new venture into fiction. My wonderful and patient sister, Carrolle Rinaldi, provided invaluable moral support as well as editing suggestions throughout the many iterations of the manuscript.

Last, but definitely not least, I thank Michael James, my publisher and the Chief Operating Officer at Fireship Press, for his enthusiasm and commitment to this project.

****

Names Cited in Text

Authentic Khmer names provided by Youk Chhang, Director of the Documentation Center of Cambodia. In the Khmer language the family name, or surname, precedes the given name. When addressing or referring to a person, the given name (rather than the family name) is used. For example, Khieu Samphan may be referred to either as Samphan or *Lok* (Mr.) Samphan.

Cheng Heng (1916–96)
After March 1970 coup led by Lon Nol and Sirik Matak, Cheng Heng, mediocre president of National Assembly, was named acting head of state.

Chh'it Chhoeun (1924–2006)
Alias "Ta Mok," commander of Khmer Rouge Southwest Zone and one of Pol Pot's most loyal and able commanders. Known as "the butcher" for his cruel methods of torturing victims.

Groslier, Bernard-Philippe (1926–86)
French scholar and archeologist who introduced modern techniques of field archeology to Cambodia in the 1950s and 1960s.

Groslier, Georges (1887–1945)
Historian and architect, he founded both the Cambodian School for the Arts and the National Museum (which he also designed) in the 1930s. Father of Bernard-Philippe Groslier.

Heng Samrin
(1934–?)

Khmer Rouge commander who fled to Vietnam in late 1970s to avoid Pol Pot's purges. Installed by Vietnamese as Cambodian head of state in 1979 and replaced by another Khmer Rouge commander, Hun Sen, in mid-1980s.

Hou Yuon
(1930–76)

Member of Cercle Marxiste as a student in Paris in the 1950s. He, along with Hu Nim and Khieu Samphan, joined Sihanouk's cabinet in 1958 but fled to Khmer Rouge jungle camps in 1967. A critic of Pol Pot's policies, he died in 1975, reportedly on the orders of Pol Pot.

Hu Nim
(1932–77)

As a student in Paris in the 1950s, he met Hou Yuon and others in Cercle Marxiste. After 1975, he became outspoken critic of Pol Pot's policies. A victim of Pol Pot's purges, he was arrested and sent to the infamous prison at Tuol Sleng. He was forced to sign a lengthy "confession" before being executed in 1977.

Hun Sen
(1952–?)

Former Khmer Rouge commander who fled to Vietnam during Pol Pot's purges. Elected Prime Minister in January 1985 and re-elected to another five-year term in July 2013. His strongman tactics, marked by corruption and alleged electoral cheating, led to widespread protests in early 2014 challenging his authoritarian rule.

Ieng Sary
(1924–2013)

Born Kim Trang. Husband of Ieng Thirith, née Khieu Thirith. Served as Vice Premier for Foreign Affairs from 1975 to 1979. Died at age 87 while awaiting trial for his Khmer Rouge activities.

Ieng Thirith
(1930–?)

Born Khieu Thirith. Younger sister of Khieu Ponnary. While in Paris, met and married Ieng Sary. She became Minister of Social Affairs in Pol Pot's government.

Jayavarman VII
(12th–13th century)

Great King of Angkor, whose reign represented zenith of Khmer empire's influence. *See* Chronology.

Kaing Guek Eav
(1942–?)

Alias "Duch." Former teacher, he ran Special Zone branch of Khmer Rouge security service, the *Santebal*. Chief of prison S-21 at Tuol Sleng.

Keng Vannsak
(1925–2008)

Cambodian scholar, philosopher, and author of dramas, plays, short stories, and poems. He mentored Pol Pot while both were in Paris in the 1950s. Shortly after, he returned to Phnom Penh where he taught at the university and at the prestigious Lycée Sisowath. He lived in exile in Paris from 1970 until his death in 2008.

Khieu Ponnary
(1920–2003)

Wife of Saloth Sar (Pol Pot). First woman to graduate from prestigious Lycée Sisowath, she met Saloth Sar in Paris, where her sister met and married Ieng Sary. President of Communist Women's Organization formed during 1960s. She suffered from chronic paranoid schizophrenia.

Khieu Samphan
(1931–?)

No relation to the sisters Khieu Ponnary and Ieng Thirith. Head of Cercle Marxiste in Paris after Ieng Sary's departure. Highly critical of Prince Sihanouk's policies, he was arrested and beaten on orders of Lon Nol. Joined Sihanouk's government but in 1967 fled to countryside with two other Khmer Rouge figures. In 1975, named principal Khmer Rouge liaison contact with Sihanouk. In 1976, Pol Pot made him head of state, but in name only.

Khieu Thirith
(1930–?)

See Ieng Thirith. Younger sister of Khieu Ponnary. While in Paris, met and married Ieng Sary and changed her name. She became Minister of Social Affairs in Pol Pot's government.

Lon Nol
(1913–85)

Defense Minister and Chief of General Staff under Sihanouk, despite having no military experience. He carried out mass murders of ethnic Vietnamese in 1970. Together with Sisowath Sirik Matak, he ousted Sihanouk in a March 1970 coup. Flown to exile in Hawaii by Americans in early April 1975, he later went to California where he died in 1985.

Lon Non
(1930–75)

Brother of Lon Nol. Known as "Little Brother," he commanded largest unit of Khmer military forces deployed around perimeter of Phnom Penh. Soon after Khmer Rouge entered the city in April 1975, he was arrested and executed by Pol Pot's men.

Mam Prum Mony (?–?) — Self-proclaimed holy man and mystic who exerted great influence over Lon Nol's political and military policies. Often referred to by Lon Nol as "the oracle," he referred to himself as the "Great Intellectual of Pure Glory."

Mouhot, Henri (1826–61) — French explorer who "discovered" ruins of Angkor Wat in 1860.

Prince Norodom Sihanouk (1922–2012) — Selected by the French to succeed King Sisowath Monivong to the throne in 1941. After a coup by Lon Nol and Prince Sisowath Sirik Matak in March 1970, Sihanouk aligned himself with the Khmer Rouge and was named head of the Khmer Rouge government in exile. Appointed King of Cambodia by Hun Sen in 1993, but with no real power.

King Norodom Suramarit (1896–1960) — Member of Norodom branch of Khmer royalty. Married to Queen Sisowath Kossamak and father of Prince (later King) Norodom Sihanouk.

Nuon Chea (1923–?) — Although considered #2 within the Khmer communist movement led by Tou Samouth, Saloth Sar (Pol Pot)—not Nuon Chea—replaced Tou Samouth after his death. Loyal deputy to Pol Pot, but defected after Pol Pot's death.

Pol Pot (1925–98) — Born Saloth Sar; also known as Brother Number One. Married Khieu Ponnary in 1956. Became leader of Cambodian Communist Party after mysterious death of previous leader, Tou Samouth. Presided over Khmer Rouge regime responsible for murders of tens of thousands suspected as traitors and almost two million others who died from forced labor, malnutrition, and lack of medicine. Arrested by rival Khmer Rouge leaders in 1998, he died of a heart attack just as he was to be brought to justice. Rumors of poisoning could not be proven since the body was cremated immediately after death.

Saloth Sar (1925–98) — See Pol Pot.

Sieu Heng (1920–75) — Former communist party official with responsibility for rural affairs, defected to Lon Nol and Sihanouk government in 1960s. Executed by Khmer Rouge shortly after they gained power.

Queen Sisowath Kossamak (1904–75)

Member of Sisowath branch of royal family. Married to King Norodom Suramarit, a member of Norodom branch of royal family. Mother of Prince Norodom Sihanouk.

King Sisowath Monivong (1896–1941)

Predecessor of Prince Norodom Sihanouk. Father of Queen Sisowath Kossamak.

Sisowath Sirik Matak (1914–75)

Cousin of Norodom Sihanouk. Chief architect of coup with Lon Nol against Sihanouk in March 1970. Sought refuge in French Embassy after Khmer Rouge entered Phnom Penh in April 1975, but executed by Khmer Rouge.

Son Sen (1927–97)

A close ally of Pol Pot, he served as Chief of Staff of Pol Pot's army and was made Minister of Defense in 1975. He came under suspicion by Pol Pot and was killed, along with his wife Yun Yat and other family members, in 1997.

Tou Samouth (1915–62)

Former Buddhist Monk and founding member of Khmer communist movement in 1951. Elected Party Secretary in 1960. Died mysteriously in 1962 and replaced by Saloth Sar (Pol Pot), who may have been implicated in death of Samouth.

Um Savuth (?–1972)

Ethnic Cham (Muslim) and General in Lon Nol's army. Chosen by Lon Nol to command the ill-fated military campaign of 1970 known as Chenla I.

Yun Yat (1937–97)

Wife of Son Sen. Minister of Culture, Education, and Propaganda in 1976.

Chronology of Khmer History

1st century   Kingdom of Funan, precursor of Khmer empire.

7th century   Khmer people conquer Funan, found Kingdom of Chenla.

8th–10th century   King Jayavarman II (reigned c.770–c.835) begins line of great kings of Angkor that lasts to mid-15th century. King Yasovarman (reigned 889–910) establishes capital at present site near town of Siem Reap.

11th century   Construction of temple at Baphuon, north of Angkor site.

12th century   Temple complex at Angkor Wat built for King Suryavarman (reigned 1113–c.1150).

1177   Chams conquer Angkor.

1181–1220   King Jayavarman VII (reigned 1181–1218 or 1220), a Buddhist, subdues Chams and builds Buddhist-inspired city of Angkor Thom and Bayon monuments.

14th–15th century   Siam sacks Angkor. Khmers abandon royal capital; in 1431, capital is moved to Phnom Penh.

17th–19th century   Khmer kingdom further diminished in battles with Siam and Vietnam, including loss to Vietnam of Cochin China (now South Vietnam).

1864   French government and Cambodian monarch sign treaty making Cambodia a French Protectorate.

early 20th century French School for Asian Studies (EFEO) begins restoration of Angkorian ruins.

1941 French select "playboy prince" Norodom Sihanouk as ruler. Japanese troops stationed in Cambodia; French remain in administrative control.

1945 End of World War II.

1951 Creation of Khmer People's Revolutionary Party, precursor to Workers' Party of Kampuchea

1954 Geneva Convention ratifies Vietnamese victory over French and divides Vietnam into pro-communist North Vietnam and pro-western South Vietnam.

1955 Sihanouk abdicates in favor of his father, King Suramarit, and forms his own political party.

1958 Sihanouk's party wins elections and begins crackdown on leftists and communists, to whom he refers pejoratively as Khmers Rouges (Red Khmers).

1960 Upon his father's death, Sihanouk names himself head of state, but retains title of Prince.

1960 First meeting of Workers' Party of Kampuchea, renamed Communist Party of Kampuchea in 1966.

1962 Death of Tou Samouth, leader of Workers' Party of Kampuchea. He is succeeded by Saloth Sar (Pol Pot) who, along with Ieng Sary, leaves for jungle areas in 1963, where they remain until 1975.

1965 Sihanouk breaks off relations with United States.

1965–1970 Khmer Rouge increase political control throughout Cambodia with support of Vietnamese communists.

1969 United States begins secret bombing raids against Vietnamese targets inside Cambodia.

1970 EFEO closes office in Siem Reap, halts restoration efforts at temple at Baphuon, and relocates to Phnom Penh.

January 6, 1970   Sihanouk travels to France for annual health cure.

March 18, 1970   Coup against Sihanouk regime is led by Lon Nol and Prince Sisowath Sirik Matak (cousin of Sihanouk).

March 23, 1970   Sihanouk, in Beijing, joins alliance with Khmer Rouge.

April 1970   Lon Nol orders mass murders of ethnic Vietnamese in Phnom Penh.

September–December 1970   Lon Nol proclaims end of Kingdom and inaugurates Khmer Republic. Lon Nol's military campaign, Chenla I, fails to reopen route to north.

January 22, 1971   Vietnamese communists attack Phnom Penh airport, virtually destroying Khmer Air Force.

February 8, 1971   Lon Nol suffers stroke, travels to Hawaii for treatment.

April 12, 1971   Lon Nol returns to Phnom Penh.

October–December 1971   Failure of Chenla II, Lon Nol's second and last attempt to reopen route to north.

March 1972   Lon Nol names himself President, Prime Minister, Defense Minister, and Marshal of the Army. United States withdraws combat troops from South Vietnam.

June 1972   Lon Nol is declared winner of first presidential elections.

August 15, 1973   U.S. Congress orders end of bombing campaign in Cambodia.

August 9, 1974   President Richard Nixon resigns.

April 1, 1975   Lon Nol resigns and goes first to Indonesia, then to Hawaii.

April 17, 1975   Khmer Rouge march into Phnom Penh and order immediate evacuation of residents.

1975–1979   Khmer Rouge policies cause deaths of up to two million people.

January 7, 1979	Vietnamese army captures Phnom Penh; Pol Pot flees to Thai border area. Vietnamese install former Khmer Rouge commander Heng Samrin as Cambodian Head of State.
1980s	Prime Minister Heng Samrin replaced by Pen Sovan who, in turn, was replaced by Hun Sen.
1991–1993	Sihanouk returns to Phnom Penh in 1991 and is granted title of King of Cambodia in September 1993. United Nations Transitional Authority in Cambodia/UNTAC (February 1992–September 1993) establishes mandates regarding human rights, elections, civil administrations, and refugee resettlement, among others.
1995	EFEO returns to Siem Reap to resume work and complete restoration of temple at Baphuon.
1996	Ieng Sary abandons Pol Pot and defects to Hun Sen. Sihanouk rewards them with land in Pailin Province.
1997–1998	Pol Pot is captured and dies in April 1998.
2011	EFEO completes restoration of 11th century temple at Baphuon.

Bibliography

Allman, T. D. "Cambodia: Nightmare Journey to a Doubtful Death." *Asia* (March–April 1982: 8–15, 52–54).

Ang Choulean. *Les Etres Surnaturels dans La Religion Populaire Khmère.* Paris: Cedoreck, 1986.

Anson, Robert Sam. *War News: A Young Reporter in Indochina.* New York: Simon & Schuster, 1989.

Asian Development Bank. *Indigenous Peoples: Ethnic Minorities and Poverty Reduction (Cambodia).* Asian Development Bank, June 2002.

Barnett, Anthony, Ben Kiernan, and Chanthou Boua. "The Bureaucracy of Death: Documents from Inside Pol Pot's Torture Machine." *New Statesman* (London, May 2, 1980).

Becker, Elizabeth. *When the War Was Over: Cambodia and The Khmer Rouge Takeover.* New York: Public Affairs, a member of the Perseus Books Group, 1988.

Bensky, Dan, and Ronald Barolet (compiled and translated by). *Chinese Herbal Medicine: Formulas and Strategies.* Seattle: Eastland Press, 1990.

Bizot, Francois. *Le Portail.* Paris: La Table Ronde, 2000.

Browne, Graeme. "Forest Stewardship in Ratanakiri: Linking Communities and Government." *Community Forestry International.* 2006.

Bullitt, John. "What is Theravada Buddhism?" www.accesstoinsight.org/lib/authors/bullitt/theravada.html. 2005.

Caldwell, Malcolm, and Lek Tan. *Cambodia in the Southeast Asian War.* New York: Monthly Review Press, 1973.

"Cambodge; Veilleur, Où En Est La Nuit?" first-hand accounts of survivors of Khmer Rouge regime prepared by Acceuil Cambodgien (Mission Catholique du Cambodge). Ateliers BREG. 30 March 1981.

Caute, David. *Communism and the French Intellectuals.* New York: Macmillan, 1981.

Chandler, David P. *Brother Number One: A Political Biography of Pol Pot.* rev. ed. Boulder: Westview Press, 1999.

Chandler, David P. "Cambodia before the French: Politics in a Tributary Kingdom 1794–1848." Doctoral Dissertation, University of Michigan, 1973.

Chandler, David P. *A History of Cambodia.* 4th. ed. Boulder: Westview Press, 2007.

Chandler, David P. *The Tragedy of Cambodian History.* New Haven: Yale University Press, 1991.

Chanrithy Him. *When Broken Glass Floats: Growing Up Under the Khmer Rouge.* New York: W.W. Norton & Company, 2000.

Coèdes, Georges. *Angkor: An Introduction. Hong Kong:* Oxford University Press, 1963.

Coomaraswamy, Ananda K. *Buddha and the Gospel of Buddha.* New York: Harper Row, 1964.

Dean, John Gunther. Oral history report of U.S. Ambassador to Cambodia (1974–75). In Frontline Democracy: The Foreign Affairs Oral History Collection of the Association for Diplomatic Studies and Training, September 2000. Filed in Jimmy Carter Presidential Library.

Ebihara, May, Carol Mortland, and Judy Ledgerwood. *Cambodian Culture since 1975.* Ithica: Cornell University Press, 1994.

Englebert, Thomas. "The Khmer in South Vietnam–Cambodians or Vietnamese?" *Nationalism and Ethnicity in Southeast Asia,* Ingrid Wessel, ed. Proceedings of the Conference on Nationalism and Ethnicity in Southeast Asia. Berlin: Humbolt University Press, October 1993. 155–196.

Etcheson, Craig. *After the Killing Fields: Lessons from the Cambodian Genocide.* Westport, Conn: Praeger, 2005.

Etcheson, Craig. "Khieu Samphan on Affairs of the Heart." *Phnom Penh Post* Issue 7/26 (November 27–December 11, 1998).

Frankland, Mark. "Witness to Bloodshed." *London Observer* (April 19, 1970).

Frieson, Kate. "In the Shadows: Women, Power and Politics in Cambodia." Centre for Asia-Pacific Initiatives, Occasional Paper No. 26. Victoria, BC, Canada. (June 2001).

Goldman, Robert P. *The Ramayana of Valmiki: An Epic of Ancient India.* Princeton: Princeton University Press, 1999.

Grant, Jonathan S., Laurance A. G. Moss and Jonathan Unger, editors. *Cambodia: The Widening War in Indochina.* New York: Washington Square Press, 1971.

Groslier, Bernard-Philippe. *Angkor: Art and Civilization.* Translated by Eric Ernshaw Smith. 1966.

Hamel, Bernard. *De Sang et De Larmes.* Paris: Albin Michel, 1977.

Hamel, Bernard. *Le Destin Khmer.* Paris: L'Harmattan, 1999.

Hamel, Bernard. "Mystery about Cambodian Communist Leader Khieu Samphan." *Reuters Dispatch* (April 24, 1974).

Hampson, Norman. *The Life and Opinions of Maximilien Robespierre.* London: Duckworth, 1974.

Headley, Robert K. Jr. *Modern Cambodian-English Dictionary.* Hyattsville, MD: Dunwoody Press, 1997.

Henley, Jon. "Thirty Years On, the Nightmare of Pol Pot's Terror Haunts Widow in Paris Suburb." *The Guardian* (January 27, 2006).

Hinton, Alexander Laban. "Agents of Death: Explaining the Cambodian Genocide in Terms of Psychological Dissonance." *Magazine of the Documentation Center of Cambodia* Numbers 31 and 32 (July–August 2002).

Hinton, Alexander Laban. *Why Did They Kill? Cambodia in the Shadows of Genocide.* Berkeley: University of California Press, 2005.

Jay, Peter. "War Tightens Grip on Phnom Penh." *New York Times Herald* (December 6, 1970).

Kamm, Henry. *Cambodia: Report from A Stricken Land.* New York: Arcade Publishing, 1998.

Kamm, Henry. "Mystic Known as the Greatest Sage of Cambodia is Said to Have Strong Influence on Premier Lon Nol." *New York Times* (October 28, 1970).

Keyes, Charles F. *Karma: An Anthropological Inquiry.* Berkeley: University of California Press, 1995.

Khieu Samphan. "Cambodia's Economic and Industrial Development." Doctoral Thesis, Sorbonne, University of Paris, 1959. Translated by Laura Summers. Ithaca: Cornell University Department of Asian Studies, 1976.

Kiernan, Ben. *How Pol Pot Came to Power; Colonialism, Nationalism, and Communism in Cambodia, 1930–1975.* Second Edition. New Haven: Yale University Press, 2004.

Kiernan, Ben. *The Pol Pot Regime: Race, Power and Genocide under the Khmer Rouge, 1975–1979.* Second Edition. New Haven: Yale University Press, 2002.

Kiernan, Ben. *The Samlaut Rebellion and its Aftermath, 1967–1970: The Origins of Cambodia's Liberation Movement.* Melbourne: Monash University Centre of Southeast Asian Studies, 1976.

Kinetz, Erika. "In Cambodia, a Clash over History of the Khmer Rouge." *Washington Post* (May 8, 2007).

Kirk, Donald. *Tell It To The Dead.* Chicago: Nelson-Hall, 1975.

Knapp, Ronald G., Jonathan Spence, and A. Chester Ong. *Chinese Houses: The Architectural Heritage of a Nation.* North Clarendon, Vermont: Tuttle Publishing, 2005.

Lefebre, Georges. *The French Revolution from 1793 to 1799*. 2 Vols. Translated by John Hall Stewart and James Friguglietti. New York: Columbia University Press, 1964.

Lon Nol. *Le Néo-Khmerisme*, revised edition. Phnom Penh: Ministry of Information, 1971.

"Lon Nol's Plans." American Embassy message to Secretary of State, Washington DC. December 1974. Declassified/Released U.S. Department of State Review, June 30, 2005.

Lowenstein, Tom. *The Vision of the Buddha: Buddhism—The Path to Spiritual Enlightenment*. New York: Barnes & Noble, 1996. (First Published in Great Britain: Macmillan Company, Ltd., 1996).

Maciocia, Giovanni. *The Foundations of Chinese Medicine: A Comprehensive Text for Acupuncturists and Herbalists*. Edinburgh: Churchill Livingstone, 1989.

Mannika, Eleanor. *Angkor Wat: Time, Space and Kinship*. Honolulu: University of Hawaii Press, 1996.

Martin, Marie Alexandrine. *Cambodia: A Shattered Society*. Translated by Mark W. McLeod. Berkeley: University of California Press, 1994.

Meyer, Charles. *Derrière Le Sourire Khmer*. Paris: Plon, 1971.

Mouhot, Henri. *Henri Mouhot's Diary: Travels in the Central Parts of Siam, Cambodia and Laos during the Years 1858–1861*. Kuala Lumpur: Oxford University Press, 1966.

Mydans, Seth. "A Top Khmer Rouge Leader Going Public, Pleads Ignorance." *Washington Post* (May 8, 2007).

Népote, Jacques. "Le Lien de Filiation au Cambodge." *Lieux de L'Enfance* No.11 (1987).

Népote, Jacques. *Parenté et Organisation Sociale dans le Cambodge Moderne et Contemporain*. Geneva: Olizane, 1992.

Ngor Haing, with Roger Warner. *A Cambodian Odyssey*. New York: Macmillan Publishing Company, 1987.

Nixon, Richard. Correspondence between U.S. President Richard Nixon and Cambodian Premier Lon Nol between 1970 and 1974. President's Personal Files, Nixon Library Holdings at National Archives, College Park, Maryland. English-French (Nixon letters) and French-English (Lon Nol letters) translations by Department of State Division of Language Services.

Osborne, Milton E. *Before Kampuchea: Preludes to Tragedy*. Boston: George Allen & Unwin, 1979.

Osborne, Milton E. *The French Presence in Cochin China and Cambodia: Role and Response (1859–1905)*. Ithica: Cornell University Press, 1969.

Osborne, Milton E. *The Mekong;Turbulent Past, Uncertain Future*. New York: Atlantic Monthly Review Press, 2000.

Pasquier, Sylvaine, and Christine Choumeau. "Cambodia in Bad Hands." *L'Express* English version (July 26, 2004): 12–18.

Phan Ana and Kevin Doyle. "Retired Ideals. Old Age Finds Ieng Sary Fully Divested of his Once Revolutionary Disdain of Wealth." *The Cambodia Daily* (October 5–6, 2002).

Ponchaud, Francois. *Year Zero*. Translated by Nancy Amphoux. New York: Holt, Rinehart & Winston, 1977.

Prud'homme, Rémy. *L'Economie du Cambodge*. Paris. 1969.

Robinson, R. H., W. L. Johnson, and Thanissaro Bhikkhu. *Buddhist Religions*. Fifth Edition. Belmont, California: Wadsworth, 2005.

Sak Sutsakhan, Lt. Gen. *The Khmer Republic at War and the Final Collapse*. Washington: U.S. Army Center for Military History, 1984.

Sarun Sar. *The Khmer Mentality*. Published as *Poloeng Khmer*, Faculty of Arts and Sciences, University of Phnom Penh, 1973. Translated by Kua Cham. Edited by Vannareth Lamm and William Snyder for the Khmer Institute. Melbourne: Khmer Aphiwath Group, 1997.

Schneberg, Willa. *Storytelling in Cambodia*. Corvallis, OR: Calyx Books, 2006.

Shaw, John M. *The Cambodian Campaign*. Lawrence: University of Kansas Press, 2005.

Shawcross, William. *The Quality of Mercy: Cambodia, Holocaust and Modern Conscience*. New York: Simon & Schuster, 1984.

Shawcross, William. *Sideshow: Kissinger, Nixon and the Destruction of Cambodia*. New York: Simon & Schuster, 1979.

Short, Philip. *Pol Pot: Anatomy of a Nightmare*. New York: Henry Holt & Company, 2004.

Sihanouk, Prince Norodom. *Les Paroles de Norodom Sihanouk*. Phnom Penh: Ministry of Information, March 1967.

Sihanouk, Prince Norodom. *War and Hope: The Case for Cambodia*. Translated by Mary Feaney, New York: Pantheon Books, 1979.

Sith Sameth. "Addressing Anarchy: Decentralization and Natural Resource Management in Ratanakiri, Upland Cambodia." *Institutions, Livelihood and the Environment*. Nordic Institute of Asian Studies, 2001.

Sok Vanny. "Réflexion sur la Khmeritude." *Asie de Sud-Est et Monde Insulindien*. II, No. 1–4 (1984).

Stuart-Fox, Martin. *The Murderous Revolution: Life and Death in Pol Pot's Kampuchea, Based on the Personal Experiences of Bunheang Ung*. Chippendale, Australia: Alternative Publishing, 1985.

Sutter, Robert G. *The Cambodian Crisis and U.S. Policy Dilemmas*. Boulder: Westview Press, 1991.

Swank, Emery. Oral history report of U.S. Ambassador to Cambodia (1971–73). In Frontline Democracy: The Foreign Affairs Oral History Collection of the Association for Diplomatic Studies and Training, January 1980.

Tarling, Nicholas. *Southeast Asia, A Modern History*. South Melbourne: Oxford University Press, 2001.

Thet Sambath. "Sister No.1. The Story of Khieu Ponnary, Revolutionary and First Wife of Pol Pot." *The Cambodia Daily* (October 20–21, 2001).

Thion, Serge. "The Pattern of Cambodian Politics." *International Journal of Politics.* 16, No. 3 (Fall 1986): 110–130.

Thion, Serge, and Ben Kiernan. *Khmers Rouges!* Paris: J.-E. Hallier/Albin Michel, 1981.

U Sam Oeur, *Sacred Vows: Poetry by U Sam Oeur*. Translated by Ken McCullough and U Sam Oeur. Minneapolis: Coffee House Press, 1998.

Van Liere, W. J. "Traditional Water Management in the Lower Mekong Basin." *World Archeology* 2/3 (1980): 265–80.

Vater, Tom. "Ratanakiri Emerges." *The Nation* (Thailand). (August 27. 2005).

Vickery, Michael. "Champa Revisited." Asia Research Institute Working Paper, No.39, 2005.

Vickery, Michael. *Kampuchea: Politics, Economics and Society*. Boulder: Lynne Rienner Publishers, Inc., 1986.

About the Author

Harriette Rinaldi

A member of the U.S. Government's Senior Executive Service and Senior Intelligence Service, Harriette Rinaldi graduated from Salve Regina University in Newport RI (B.A)

and received her Master's Degree from Brown University. She also pursued graduate studies at the Sorbonne in Paris.

During her twenty-seven-year career with the Central Intelligence Agency, she enjoyed challenging overseas assignments involving the collection of foreign intelligence responsive to the needs of American policy makers, and served in several leadership positions at Headquarters. She was the founder of CIA's Women's Leadership Forum and a regular speaker at interagency conferences and policy forums. She has received many awards from CIA and other U.S. Government entities. After retirement, she taught leadership seminars for mid- and senior-level government managers throughout the country, including specialized training programs for NASA, the Department of Justice, and the U.S. Army Special Forces. She is the author of a nonfiction book entitled *Born at the Battlefield of Gettysburg: An African-American Family Saga* published in 2005 (Markus Wiener Publishers, Princeton NJ).

If You Enjoyed This Book
You'll Find More to Love Printed
by

FIRESHIP PRESS
www.fireshippress.com

Fireship Press books are available directly through our website, amazon.com, Barnes and Noble and Nook, Sony Reader, Apple iTunes, Kobo books and via leading bookshops across the United States, Canada, the UK, Australia and Europe.

The Unmarked Road

by

George Cadwalader

Marine Gunnery Sergeant John "K-Bar" Caleb has survived everything the Viet Nam War could throw at him, as his many Bronze Stars attest. He has been one of the most admired, and the most feared man of his unit, until a grenade explosion sends him to Philadelphia's Naval Hospital. There he violently relives his battles in recurring nightmares, undermining the doctors' efforts to save his mangled arm and hand.

In a final gamble Caleb is sent for treatment to the hospital's psych ward, where the windows are barred and the walls show marks where men before him have tried to claw their way out. To regain his life again, Caleb must come to terms with everything he has seen, everything he has done, and all that he has lost in a prolonged conflict between conviction and conscience.

Fireship Press
www.FireshipPress.com

WWW.FIRESHIPPRESS.COM
HISTORICAL FICTION AND NONFICTION
PAPERBACK AVAILABLE FOR ORDER ON LINE
AND AS EBOOK WITH ALL MAJOR DISTRIBUTERS

God Does Not Forget

by

Deneys Reitz

"One of the greatest war books ever written."
"A vivid, unforgettable picture of mobile guerrilla warfare."

In 1899 a 17 year old boy by the name of Dennys Reitz volunteered to fight for his country, South Africa, against the British. He could ride and shoot with the best of them, so he was quickly assigned to a Boer Commando Unit—one of the highly mobile light cavalry units that were driving the British crazy. Outmanned, outgunned, and under-supplied, the Boer commandos nevertheless checked the British at almost every turn. They became masters of lightning attacks, night fighting, and ambushes, only to disappear to strike again somewhere else.

Reitz was in it from beginning to end, and participated in nearly every major battle. His descriptions of war and adventure have come to be regarded as among the best in the English language.

After the fighting was over, Reitz chose to live in Madagascar rather than remain in South Africa under British rule; and it was from there that he wrote this book. But his exile did not last. His old commander talked him into returning to his homeland to help build the new dominion. To this task, he brought the courage and leadership he had learned as a commando, eventually becoming a Member of Parliament, Cabinet Minister, Deputy Prime Minister, and South African High Commissioner to London. He also fought bravely on the Western Front during WW-I—for the British.

Fireship Press
www.FireshipPress.com

www.Fireshippress.com
Found in all leading Booksellers and on line
eBook distributors

SMART AND FAITHFUL FORCE

by

JAMES HOLDEN-RHODES

"HE WAS A REMARKABLE MAN...HE WAS 'ORNERY' AND MEANER THAN HELL..."

"James Holden-Rhodes has written a superb account of the life and contributions of a truly fascinating character in the history of our nation and the Marine Corps. It is the brilliantly told and researched story of Henry Clay Cochrane , a hero, reformer and innovator....a must read for those interested in understanding the historical evolution of the Marine Corps into the renowned fighting force it has become....

"Jim Holden-Rhodes rescues the history of the Marine Corps from the post-Civil War "dark Ages' or organizational stagnation. The career of Henry Clay Cochrane shows that a few brave reformers pushed the Marine Corps to higher standards of appearance, discipline, training and marksmanship. As it entered its imperial years, 1898-1933, the Marine Corps showed that its soaring self esteem was justified by its fighting skills. Cochrane showed the way."

Allan R. Millett, author of *Semper Fidelis: The History of the United States*

Fireship Press
www.FireshipPress.com

www.Fireshippress.com
Found in all leading Booksellers and on line
eBook distributors

In Kon Tiki's Wake

by

P.J Capelotti

It was the original Survivor series, only without the omnipresent cameras, paramedics, and faux tribal rituals. Between the spring of 1947 and the summer of the year 2006, more than forty expeditions sought to drift across the oceans of the world on rafts. These audacious voyages began with the legendary Kon-Tiki expedition, under the leadership of the renowned Norwegian explorer Thor Heyerdahl. The Kon-Tiki raft drifted more than four thousand miles from Peru to Polynesia, and remained afloat months after experts predicted it would sink to the bottom of the Pacific. Heyerdahl's radical thesis of a prehistoric world where ancient mariners drifted between continents on ocean currents electrified the postwar world. His Kon-Tiki: Across the Pacific by Raft sold twenty million copies in sixty-five languages.

In the wake of Kon-Tiki documents all of the transoceanic raft expeditions that were organized and carried out in the half century after Kon-Tiki. Spanning more than fifty years and recounting more than forty expeditions, In the wake of Kon-Tiki is a riveting chronicle of human daring, endurance, and folly.

Fireship Press
www.FireshipPress.com

www.Fireshippress.com
Found in all leading Booksellers and on line
eBook distributors

CPSIA information can be obtained
at www.ICGtesting.com
Printed in the USA
FSOW02n2026230117
29969FS